SIX DEGREES of EXPATRIATION

Uncovering the lives of expats in Singapore

Marshall Cavendish Editions

Published by Marshall Cavendish Editions
An imprint of Marshall Cavendish International
1 New Industrial Road, Singapore 536196

Other Marshall Cavendish Offices

Marshall Cavendish Ltd. 5th Floor 32–38 Saffron Hill, London EC1N 8FH, UK • Marshall Cavendish Corporation. 99 White Plains Road, Tarrytown NY 10591-9001, USA • Marshall Cavendish International (Thailand) Co Ltd. 253 Asoke, 12th Flr, Sukhumvit 21 Road, Klongtoey Nua, Wattana, Bangkok 10110, Thailand • Marshall Cavendish (Malaysia) Sdn Bhd, Times Subang, Lot 46, Subang Hi-Tech Industrial Park, Batu Tiga, 40000 Shah Alam, Selangor Darul Ehsan, Malaysia

Marshall Cavendish is a trademark of Times Publishing Limited

National Library Board Singapore Cataloguing in Publication Data

Pineda, Maida C.
Six degrees of expatriation : uncovering the lives of expats in Singapore / by Maida C. Pineda. – Singapore : Marshall Cavendish Editions, c2009.
p. cm.
ISBN-13 : 978-981-4276-67-2

1. Aliens – Singapore – Anecdotes. 2. Aliens – Singapore – Social life and customs.
3. Singapore – Social life and customs. I. Title.

DS609.9
305.90691095957 -- dc22   OCN430797447

Printed in Singapore by Fabulous Printers Pte Ltd

For my father,
Dr. Florencio Pineda

Thank you for introducing me to the
gift of travel at such a young age.
Dad, at age five you taught me to capture
the joy of being in a different culture.
By teaching me to write a simple journal
in a small spiral notebook,
And showing me how to take pictures
with an instamatic camera,
You gave me the tools for savoring my trips.
In every photo you took of us against a wonderful view,
You always teased me and my siblings that we were just props,
The real star was the view behind us.
Thanks for reminding me not to lose
sight of what is really important.
I love you more than my words and actions can show.

Contents

With Thanks And Appreciation

Three days after I arrived in Singapore, I was distressed with the bleak prospects of my house hunting at a time when rent was at its peak. I went to Kinokuniya, a gigantic bookstore on Orchard Road, seeking solace in books. I felt right at home reading Moving On, the latest book by my favourite author, Sarah Ban Breathnach. She writes:

"It doesn't matter whom you live with or where you move from or to,
you always take yourself with you. If you don't know who you are,
or if you've forgotten or misplaced her,
then you'll always feel as if you don't belong. Anywhere."

Coming to Singapore, making it home, and writing this book has been nothing less than a journey. It is a journey to a foreign land, a journey to find a home, a journey to find love, a journey to belong to a community, a journey of faith, a journey of friendship, and a journey within. Thankfully, I am not alone in this adventure.

Many thanks to:

Sr. Bubbles, r.c.—for daring me to go on a food trip to

Singapore. Who would have known this eating binge would turn into a life-changing trip? I'm sure you knew. You have journeyed with me for eleven years as a spiritual director, an eating buddy, an older sister, and most importantly a dear friend. You have always seen the goodness and beauty in me, and constantly dared me to become a better person.

The Cenacle Sisters (Sr. Fran, Sr. Mel, Sr. Anelie, and Sr. Marido)—for opening their home to this homeless writer when I arrived. You not only opened the door to your house, but also opened your hearts to me.

Elizabeth—for sharing a warm and cozy tropical home in the heartlands with me. Thank you for choosing me as your flatmate. It is such a joy to live with a fellow single, spunky single woman. It is great to have each other to vent about bad days, dating disasters or the few dating successes, share enlightened realizations, music, travels, silky chocolate pudding, and even the sniffles.

To the baristas of the former Starbucks at Raffles Place (across Chijmes)—not only did you make the best velvety foam I desired for my cappuccino, you also offered the best service in Singapore. When you saw me, you happily greeted me with a smile, handed me a glass of ice water to cool me down, and made sure I got my favorite writing table. It was like I had an office, minus the office politics. You gave me the much-needed perk on days I was down with a broken heart, or suffered writer's block. You told me your stories and your dreams, and you really cared how I was doing. More than just familiar strangers, you treated me as a friend. Thanks!

Chiquit, Shawn and Manny were my first friends here in Singapore, and instantly they became my family here. Chiquit helped me to get settled, with priceless tips, information, and getting me organized with the handy street directory and bus guide. She patiently answers my 101 questions, and boards the first bus to console me in desperate times. She is my frequent Sunday brunch buddy. Shawn is my cool as cucumber buddy. We've had our nature adventures and long dinners. But I will never forget how you patiently listened as I was sobbing for a lost love in a park in Bishan. And my dear, dear Manny, it is hard to imagine life in Singapore without you. We've made countless memories around this island together. From the first time we conversed in bus 174, to discovering cheap and cheerful meals, a spa trip to Batam, visiting seven churches in one night by foot and MRT, sharing dreams and love stories. Whether I was lamenting why I got talked into getting bangs, or what dress to wear to my sister's wedding, or even life's more profound problems, you were always there for me. Thanks beyond words!

To the FX choir—for sharing with me the gift of song and faith.

And to my family, who has always supported me in whatever I do. My sister, Rissa, thanks for letting me take over your third floor for one month, converting it into a writer's studio as I hibernated to finish this book.

Mom and dad, your deep love continues to give me the strength to pursue my dreams. Thank you for the lovely home I grew up in Manila. But you also gave me wings to find my home in the world. I love you!

Lastly, this book would not have been possible without the expats who generously shared their life stories. They opened up and trusted me with the intimate details of their lives. Scott, Rachel, John, Shawn, Sarah, Steve, Margaret, Guillaume, the Thai ladies who lunch, Rom, Alex, Giovanni, and Kiran, how happy I am that Singapore is a compact society and that our paths have crossed. Thank you for enriching my life, and those who will read your stories!

Part

I

MY STORY

01 *Life is What Happens When You are Busy Making Plans*

John Lennon could not have captured it better than his words "Life is what happens when you are busy making plans." Life has a funny way of turning out. As much as I love writing lists, dreaming, and scribbling five- and ten-year plans, at the end of the day, life has its unique way of unfolding. I never really planned to move to Singapore and call it home. But my life has been a delicious adventure that unfolds in a rather colourful way.

I moved to Singapore a year and a half ago. But the story really began two years ago. I am a food and travel writer, who was born and raised in the Philippines. With a voracious appetite for adventure, the whole archipelago of 7,107 islands became my great big classroom of learning. Well, it was more of a playground of connecting and conversing with people and re-telling their story through my articles. I indulged in this wanderlust, learning as much as I could about food and travel until I received a scholarship to study my Masters in Gastronomy in Adelaide, Australia. This extended my classroom and playground to a great big world outside the Philippines. After finishing my Masters in Adelaide, I considered moving to Sydney or

Singapore. But in the end, I moved back home to Manila. I returned to my life of writing food and travel articles for magazines. My job ranged from searching for noteworthy restaurants around the archipelago to experiencing the country's best surfing destination to finding remote beaches. But at this point having done most of the best attractions in the country, I was raring for a new adventure.

One of my little joys is finding small hole-in-the-wall eateries serving delicious food. I would share my discoveries with my dearest friends. As I was eating grilled pork in a tiny kitchenette in the suburb of Quezon City, my companion Sr. Bubbles, a Catholic nun and fellow foodie, verbalized her dream, "Maida, it would be so nice if we could do a food trip in Singapore." She mentioned having a retreat scheduled in Kuala Lumpur, Malaysia, in March. At that time, the Philippines was enjoying the entry of budget airlines, with aggressive marketing and sales promotions to lure travelers to local and international destinations. Taking advantage of one of these sales, I found cheap tickets to Malaysia to coincide with my friend's schedule. We figured we would take the coach from KL to Singapore together. Not having been to KL before, I organized to meet up with a friend's friend who happily showed me around the pockets of his hometown.

Sr. Bubbles and I met at the bus terminal at KL and took the bus to Singapore. When we got off the bus in Novena and hopped into a cab, only then did it dawn on us. We had actually executed our little dream. I stayed in a convent in Jurong West, along with my friend and her fellow nuns. I also arranged to conduct some interviews with some Filipino hoteliers working in Singapore for an article I was writing for an in-flight magazine of a budget airline.

It wasn't my first time in Singapore. In November 1994, I had stopped by for an overnight stay on my way back home to Manila from Perth, Australia, where I was an exchange student for one semester. My Catholic dormitory had a good number of Singaporean students and I became particularly close to James and Yvette. Both happily showed me the country during my brief visit. Yvette made sure I tucked into authentic local hawker food. I distinctly recall James and I taking the MRT, where we did a little sociological experiment. We stood by the door, watching people file out of the train, and we smiled at everyone, waiting to see who would smile back at us. And sadly, not a single person smiled back at us. It proved the point James was trying to make, that no one smiles in Singapore. With a laid-back and relaxed demeanor, James had obviously taken on the Aussie ways.

But that was 13 years ago. Much has happened to the Lion City and to my life as well. I returned to Singapore with fresh eyes. My friend, Sr. Bubbles, just loved Singapore. She feels on guard going around in Malaysia, but once she steps foot onto Singapore, she relaxes and feels very much at home.

That trip had a three-fold purpose: to enjoy the food offerings of Singapore with my friend, to work on my article about Filipino hoteliers, and to explore the possibility of working here. Everything seemed exotic, I even marveled at the brisk hand movement of the Indian man preparing the crispy *roti prata* at Upper Thomson. His head bobbed while he made this flat bread and I took a video of his culinary artistry. I was in awe, through my eyes, everything seemed fresh and new. I also thoroughly enjoyed partaking of Singapore standards like Hainanese chicken rice and oyster omelet. But what amazed me most was how productive my days were. In one day, I could easily manage doing three interviews. This was a struggle in Manila, where just driving from my home to Makati and finding parking was an ordeal on its own. In Singapore, getting around is a breeze on a cab or MRT, considering I was even staying in the far western end of Jurong. And in the lives of the Filipinos I interviewed, I got a glimpse of what it was like to live in Singapore. Their lives were not perfect, but it was evident they enjoyed being here.

I also met up with Chiquit, whom I worked with on a home design magazine in the Philippines many years back. She had moved to Singapore for over two years now, and was working full-time with a design magazine here. She too was satisfied with her life in Singapore.

Believing in seasons and times in our lives, I sensed it was time to move from the Philippines, and Singapore was the logical bet.

02

My Life in a 25-Kilo Suitcase

Five months later, I arrived in Singapore on 23 August 2007. The date is clearly etched in my memory. I struggled packing my life into a 25-kilo suitcase allowed by the airline. But somehow, I managed to begin my life with just the basics. Arriving at about three in the afternoon, walking out of Changi Airport Terminal 1, I could distinctly feel the humidity. I was expecting it to be just as humid as my beloved Philippines, only to realise it was more humid. Even just standing merits a stream of perspiration to form. I easily caught a cab for my long drive from Changi all the way to Jurong West. I was headed to a convent, where the kind nuns of the Religious of the Cenacle had allowed me to stay with them for a few days until I found a place to rent. They had rooms available for retreats, but luckily at this time there were no retreatants staying with them.

As soon as I got in the cab, the driver engaged me in conversation, asking where I was from. Little did I know, conversing with cab drivers would be a regular fixture of my life in Singapore. When he found out I was from the Philippines, he told me his girlfriend was Filipina too. But there seemed to be complications. She had another man and a family left back home. He was so excited and called his girlfriend, then handed his mobile phone to me. Not really sure what to say to this Filipina, I made small talk for a minute or so, then handed the phone back to the driver. By the time, I got to the convent, I was disoriented. I recall standing by the door holding my suitcases, feeling very much like Maria of *The Sound of Music*, seeking refuge with the nuns.

They welcomed me with so much warmth. It was a diverse community of four nuns: one Filipino nun in her forties, one Filipino nun in her sixties from the US, a French nun, and the lone Singaporean nun in the order. They offered me some tea and biscuits, telling me of the barbecue they had organized that evening in the compound for their neighbor, a nun leaving for her mission work.

Journal Entry

23 August 2007: Gate Crasher

I arrived at Singapore some five hours ago. But in that short span of time, I have already started my adventure. A cab driver upon finding out I was Filipina told me about his girlfriend of four years, Gemma. He lamented how he bought her and her family four cellphones, yet she still won't pick up the phone when she is home in the Philippines. He called her naughty, pertaining to the possibility of this woman having a husband back home. He even called her and let her talk to me. As I paid my cab fare, he scribbled her number just in case I wanted to call her.

I am staying at Cenacle, a convent and retreat house. I am friends with the nuns here. Since it is a retreat house, they have rooms to spare and have kindly allowed me to stay here while I search for an apartment. Sr. Mel told me my timing was perfect as there was a barbecue tonight for their neighbors. They are in a compound of Catholic religious orders. In fact, I felt very much like Maria von Trapp, standing by the door with my overweight suitcase, ringing the doorbell.

I love barbecues. It is huge in Australia. But this would have to be the most Asian barbecue I've had. Unlike the usual, sausages and salads, there was a huge container of *beehoon*, thin rice noodles with a satay sauce. There was *sotong* (squid), sausages, marshmallows, prawns, satay sticks, and chicken wings.

The squid was tender with a tinge of sweetness, perfect when dipped in the satay sauce. The head of the *sotong* when grilled to a crunch bursts into an explosion of flavor in my mouth. Ignatius, the only little boy in the group, had a blast roasting marshmallows on sticks for all the nuns.

And for dessert, there were tubs of ice cream from Island Creamery. The flavors were unique, like Tiger Beer. It tasted like an icy pint of beer, a light sorbet capturing the foamy beer taste. My favorite was Horlicks, a creamy rendition of my childhood favorite malt candy.

While the nuns were engaged in friendly chatter, loud noises started. It was the Festival of the Hungry Ghosts*, they explained. Gongs clanged loudly just behind the compound. I grabbed my camera and headed there to see what the ruckus was all about. A huge tent was laid out and a celebration of sorts was ongoing.

I watched the makeshift outdoor kitchen prepare lavish platters. There were about a hundred people waiting to be served their dinner. Occasionally they would hold a stick of incense and bow towards the three gigantic candles. There was a puppet show. Behind the curtains was a man alternating between sipping his Tiger beer and puffing his stick of cigarette. There were women with no script acting out the lines of the puppet show into the mike.

There was no one to ask what was going on for I was merely gatecrashing.

The fatigue of the long day packing and traveling crept up on me. The nuns were still enjoying tea, but I excused myself to rest. Outside my window, the gongs were still clanging with loud chants I could not understand. It sounded like a Chinese movie on television. I tried to tune it out…until I fell asleep at last.

*It is a month-long festival, which takes place during the 7th lunar month. It is believed that during this time, souls are released from Purgatory to wander the earth for a month. During this month, activities include Taoist monks chanting, preparing ritualistic food offerings and burning incense and joss papers for the visiting spirits. There is also a *getai*, a boisterous live stage performance. The backdrop of the stage is made of brightly-colored cardboard, with performers wearing vibrant costumes too.

In the days that followed, I no longer felt like a gatecrasher. I took the MRT on my own. I dined alone in the hawker center in Jurong having a bowl of chicken curry noodles. But it was too spicy for my taste buds and I drowned it with a glass of lime juice. Filipinos are spice wimps, with a very low tolerance for hot food. Later, the vendor walked to my table asking if I found it too spicy and I said yes. He said, "You Filipino? You should just eat chicken rice all the time." The sight of tropical fruits in the market fascinated me: spiky, stinky durians, massive pomelos, a strange looking fruit similar to the jackfruit which I later learn is called champedak, and shocking pink dragon fruits. As I wandered around the market, Sr. Fran, the Singaporean nun, spotted me. She showed me a store selling incense, paper money and other paper effigies like paper houses, paper cameras, paper cellphones, and other paper appliances that the dead will need in their journey to the afterlife. There were packets of cooked food on the ground with incense offered for the dead during the Hungry Ghost season. Taking my immersion into Chinese culture one step further, Sr. Fran brought me to a Chinese wedding store also located in the market in Jurong West. An old man showed me everything a bride needed: slippers, basins, containers, and red things with double happiness inscribed on them. Sr. Fran said, "Just in case you marry a Chinese, I'll be your godmother." I was overwhelmed.

My adventures continued every day. Everything seemed fresh and new. I talked to people, asking questions. I was curious. I talked to Enzo, the guy who made pancakes filled with cheese, chocolate, and peanut flavors, about his product. Sr. Mel was certain I'd make a good reality TV show. She imagined how fun it would be to have a camera attached to me, capturing my everyday adventures.

03

Finding a Place to Call My Home

Looking for a place to stay was quite challenging. I had it clear in my head that I would spend only a few days in the convent, not wanting to be a burden to the nuns. It should not exceed a week, I promised myself. Sr. Mel, the Filipino nun in her forties, put aside the classifieds for me. I walked over to 7-11 to purchase a SIM card, and I was in business. I then made my calls to the prospective places in the classifieds. But I was shocked with the phone etiquette of the agents. There was no "hello" when they picked up their phones, only a direct question, "How much your budget?" Then when I quoted my minimal budget for a room, they would often hang up without even saying goodbye. I thought it was rather harsh. Coming from a culture of warm and friendly people, this was a drastic change. Even without seeing their eyes, I could almost imagine the dollar sign flashing in them.

Upon the advice of a friend, I checked out the rooms for rent on singaporeexpats.com, a website for expats in Singapore. I narrowed it down to two choices. One was a HDB unit near Buona Vista, the other was a condominium near Holland Village. With the assistance of Sr. Fran, I learnt how to get there using the MRT and a cab. It was not exactly accessible by public transport but I still made it to the condominium. It was a three-bedroom unit. The master bedroom was occupied by a Chinese lady working for an IT company. I was to share a bathroom with a French lady who had just arrived. The room was decent sized, but with a small window. And it was on a very high floor, making my knees go weak when I walked along the corridor heading to the lift. I knew this could be a problem if I had a drink. I soon realized it was hard to get around from here, and I will probably have to rely on cabs. It was not ideal for someone starting out in Singapore with minimal funds.

I then checked out the HDB unit, where I would have to share the place with a Filipina dentist. It was a two-bedroom unit with one bathroom we had to share. That didn't score well in my books. She told me she used to work long hours until 11 in the night, oftentimes with no lunch break. I asked if people had their teeth checked till that late, and she nodded with sadness. But she will start working with a foreign dentist with more manageable work hours. She had dreams of moving to Australia, so she was studying for the board exams during her spare time. The price was affordable, but I didn't get a good vibe. She worried that I was not a Permananent Resident like her, explaining that was what her landlord preferred. I also felt like I was moving into her place, rather than living in our place. She explicitly said she was fussy about cleanliness. This artist is no stickler for being organized. This could be a huge problem if I had to share a bathroom with her. I was also not comfortable having people look into my room as they made their way to the common lift. Like most HDB residents, she used a big padlock for the grills, locking herself in the unit. It made me feel cooped up, like a prison.

I also checked out a unit at River Valley Road, recommended by a Filipino acquaintance. It was the rich Chinese owner's Filipino maid who took care of leasing her units. She had keys to the multiple units of her boss and she showed me into the different units. Walking inside the first one, I was shocked to see a shrine with the owner's ancestor's photo and some oranges. I was not sure I was comfortable to see that image everyday. The maid said there were Filipinos renting the rooms. They were entertainers, singers in a band. She showed me the second unit, which was a studio unit. Nice, but beyond my budget. The third option was a house about to be renovated. There were several foreign tenants staying on for the last few weeks. I could stay there for a few days until I found a place.

On the third day of my search for a place to stay, I took a break and headed to Kinokuniya on Orchard Road. I found refuge in the company of books; there's nothing more soothing for this writer than the scent of new books. I got lost in the countless options available, the store was so huge and I spent hours pouring through the books. One of the books I chose to buy was called *Moving On*. This collection of essays by Sarah Ban Breathnach was an apt companion to this new phase in my life. Clutching the books I wanted to purchase, I received a phone call. A perky American was on the line. "Are you still looking for a room to rent?" she asked. I answered her with another question, "Where is it?" "Ang Mo Kio," she answered. I had no clue where that was. It was not on my radar. But I asked another important question, "Do I have to share a bathroom?" "No, you have your own bathroom." Those were the magic words I needed to hear. I didn't care where Ang Mo Kio was. I agreed to see the place an hour or so later. The caller, Elizabeth, said she was going for a run, but would be back in time for our agreed meeting.

I took the MRT to Yio Chu Kang. Good feelings were brewing within me. I finally succumbed to an ice cream treat to beat the heat. Just outside the MRT were two ice cream vendors selling Magnolia ice cream. The vendor used an extra sharp knife to cut the ice cream into inch-thick bricks, then put them in between a pastel-colored bread. It became an instant ice cream sandwich. I chose a flavor I would never have chosen before, mint chocolate chip, hoping the minty flavour would refresh me from the humidity.

I then began looking for this condominium. I was utterly confused why the streets were all the same. Ang Mo Kio Avenue 6, Ang Mo Kio Avenue 8, then Ang Mo Kio Street 61. Why couldn't they have different names, I thought to myself. I got over the confusion, and made my way to the condomium. It was a 10- to 15-minute walk from the MRT, located next to a hospital. I asked the security guards about the unit number, and they knew this American girl. It was a walk-up apartment with three floors amidst a condominium complex with several pale pink painted buildings, some walk-up units, and other high rises with lifts. The neighbors had their shoes stacked on shoe racks outside their door. Apparently, most homes in Singapore practice a no-shoe policy inside their homes to keep it clean.

I arrived and found the wooden door opened and the grills locked. This allowed me to get a glimpse of the place. There was no one in sight, but I could hear the water running in the shower. In a few minutes, a tall, skinny lady came out of the shower with a big, bright smile. She welcomed me into her home and offered me a glass of cold water from her empty fridge. We started talking in the kitchen. She was an international schoolteacher, and I explained I was a food and travel writer. She gushed about how she loved to eat and travel. In fact, she had been to the Philippines several times.

She was a seasoned backpacker. What was intended to be a quick five-minute look-see lasted for over an hour. We shared about each other's lives. She showed me the room, which was an empty but large room with a queen size bed. It had the basics, A/C and a wardrobe. And the best part was I had my own bathroom.

She told me she turned on her computer and saw my posting on singaporeexpats.com, where I expressed I was a 32-year-old journalist looking for a room to rent. She said she initially planned to use this room as her guest room. The flat was an unfurnished rental, which was over her budget. She cleverly furnished it with second-hand furniture from teachers who were relocating and some bits from Ikea. The living room had one wall painted a nice deep red, which provided a great contrast with the black leather couch. There were several plants on the balcony, creating a tropical feel suited for this island girl. Elizabeth's room was painted a creamy butter yellow, just like my room in Manila. She said she had painted all this by herself. I was impressed. I told her I was considering a place in Holland Village and would like to think about it. She said she did not have time to look for a tenant for she was a busy teacher who spent long hours at work.

Elizabeth walked me to see the pool and the gym as I headed out. I went back to the convent telling the nuns of my wonderful find over dinner. There was positive energy all around the dinner table. When I finally went back to my room, I found a message from Elizabeth offering to lower the rent. She told me she just wanted me to be her roommate. I followed my gut feeling and agreed immediately.

And in three short days, I found my home in Singapore. I moved two days later. Sally, a kind friend from grad school with a classy white Mercedes Benz, offered to take me to Ikea to buy some essentials for my room, like bed sheets, a desk lamp, bath mats, trashcans, hangers, and a laundry basket. We then brought it straight to my new room. After that, I took a cab with my 25-kilo suitcase from Jurong to my new home in Yio Chu Kang, starting life anew.

Soon after, this writer found her peace. I knew I was home for I could happily write in this new environment. During the daytime, I sat at the dining room table where I could see the plants, with birds stopping by to sing me a melodic tune. I could hear the maid from two floors down belting Mariah Carey and other powerful songs lamenting lost loves and lovers far away. I could only imagine why she sang these songs with such intense emotion, perhaps the sadness of being far away from her one true love in the Philippines. I assumed her boss was away at this time of the day, and she could happily sing to her heart's content. There were many Filipinos and Indonesians working as domestic helpers in our condominium complex.

Our kitchen extended to a utility area where we did our laundry. It had a grill and windows looking out to the parking lot. Parked down below were a merry mix of Mercedes Benz and BMWs. I was shocked to discover the maids cleaning the cars at 11 pm or even later. Other maids had a routine of cleaning their bosses' cars in the morning at 6 or 7 am before they went off for work.

I was then in a honeymoon stage with Singapore. Everything was neat and organized. The MRT was my best friend, as there was no way one could get lost. I immediately memorized the stops on the red line. When riding the train, I had a good look at the HDB buildings. It looked like Lego-land to me, and it felt like I was not living a real life—rather I became one of those plastic people living on an architect's model. Everything seemed so symmetric. It was worlds apart from the streets of Manila, where order was scarce, and there were numerous squatters' makeshift dwellings made of galvanized sheets, pieces of scrap wood, and the mandatory tire on the roof, just so it wouldn't fly off when the typhoons came. Here there was no litter, and no sign of beggars.

With my home situation settled, I could now concentrate on my work situation. I arrived with an approval for EPEC, allowing me to stay to look for work for one year. Prior to moving to Singapore, I was already writing for several editors in this Lion city. But this time I was looking for a full-time job, instead of merely contributing stories for magazines.

After One Month in Singapore
A Letter to My Loved Ones Back Home
20 September 2007, 10 am

"We can travel a long way and do many different things, but our deepest happiness is not born from accumulating new experiences. It is born from letting go of what is unnecessary, and knowing ourselves to always be at home." — *Sharon Salzburg*

Exactly four weeks ago today I left home. I left my family, my friends, and my dogs in the Philippines. It is a country that I have always known to be home. I genuinely love the warmth and quirkiness of the Filipinos. I always marvel at how gorgeous the archipelago is. And I can say that with much authority, having traveled to majority of the provinces in the country as a travel writer. I had left home many times for brief work trips or to study abroad. But this time, I chose to move to Singapore to work and to give myself a better life.

When I'm asked why I wanted to leave, I explained it best using an analogy. I described living in the Philippines for me as old chewing gum, the gum that you have chewed out all the juices and it has become hard from all your chewing. Pretty much like an overchewed Juicy Fruit Gum. Having covered almost all the big travel stories and restaurants in the country, it had become too easy and too comfortable. It was the same old thing. I wanted something I could sink my teeth into. Something more stimulating. I also realized that I did not like the lifestyle in Manila. I wanted to be more hands-on to cook for myself, to be more independent, and not to get too tired driving or finding parking. Yes, I longed for a developed country with a system that works. In the past few years, I learned that life isn't easy. And if day to day things like traffic or inefficient service, or poor systems, take its toil on you and prevent you from living your best life, perhaps it is best to find the place that does. Here, I can enjoy the ease of getting around, finding an apartment, being taken care of by the law even without a lawyer, getting your deposit on the day you vacate your apartment, and getting things done online. I also wanted to provide for myself a better future. I'm in my thirties, and while I love being immersed in my passions—food, travel and writing—it is time to make sure I get compensated properly and save for my future. Since writing doesn't pay well, I always used to joke that I will just marry rich to support my craft. I now realize I must be the best in my craft so I can live comfortably and with much joy.

So I left home, limiting my life to the allocated 20 kilos allowed by the budget airline. I had no job, no place to stay, and limited funds. Four weeks later, I happily reside in this most wonderful condominium with a pool, a gym, and a gorgeous koi pond. My apartment is spacious and has been referred to by a visiting friend as an IKEA showroom. It is lush with lots of plants, making me feel right at home, bringing back memories of our large garden at home. And I share the place with Elizabeth, an American schoolteacher two years my junior. She has the kindest heart, and is extremely wholesome.

It was frightening to move in with a total stranger. But you know in your heart instantly when you've found a friend. We are kindred spirits. We both love the color orange, tofu, cheese, chocolate, comfortable ugly shoes, plants, and traveling around Asia. We even wear the same size shoes. And, with each day, we realize we have more things in common, but are different enough to make our friendship colorful. She is a healthy vegetarian who goes for long runs, is very conscious about making choices good for the environment, and does not watch TV. In fact we do not have one in our apartment. She is all together wholesome. On the other hand, I can't live without meat. I have no second thoughts about going to Starbucks, even if it's a big corporation. I probably use too much paper towel and paper. But yes, I do try to recycle. And it is the first time in my life I am living without a television.

It has been exactly four weeks without a TV. And, yes, I can proudly say I survived! There are days when I would have severe withdrawals, surfing the websites of *Oprah*, *Ellen*, *Grey's Anatomy*, and some reality TV shows I was once addicted to.

The hours I used to veg in front of the television seems like a whole lifetime ago.

So one month later, I no longer feel like I am chewing the hard gum devoid of flavor. I am now chewing a softer gum bursting with flavor, perhaps too much flavor! I am stimulated by the new adventures: the new experiences, new dishes to try, new places to see, new people to talk to. It is not familiar, and that excites me. However I have found what is familiar in Singapore as well: friends, Filipinos, the kindness of people no matter what race, gorgeous sunny days, good coffee, enjoying my own company, a nice swim, the list goes on...

In a month, I have accomplished much. I've let go of many attachments at home. I have found a lovely place in Singapore, and I have made it home. I have made friends. I have found contacts. I have impressed some editors and even secured some assignments. I've had a lot of laughs. I've done things I would have never done before, like put together an electric fan all by myself, or live a month without TV. I've walked countless steps and mastered the MRT. Hey, I can even recite the stops along the red line (North-South line). I've gone to three different churches, watched a duck race, and attended a cooking class. I am slowly becoming familiar with the hawker dishes. But I have yet to understand Singlish. I've sprained my ankle and am learning to take care of it, and have become patient with my slower pace. And, most of all, I am happy. That's quite an achievement for a month. And the quote by Sharon Salzberg captures the entire feeling I have. Truly, for no matter where I go, I know I will always be home.

04 *The Fall*

Getting my papers sorted out required a visit to the ICA (Immigrations and Checkpoints Authority) just outside Lavender MRT. Having wine with a friend one evening, his friend learned I was a food writer and suggested I sample soup *tulang*, a mutton bone marrow you had to suck with a straw. It was a delicacy I could find in the Golden Mile Complex, within walking distance from the ICA. After all the nitty-gritty paperwork, I was issued my lovely green EPEC card. Apparently this was essential in getting anything done in Singapore. Rejoicing over my little accomplishment, I then headed to Golden Mile to find this *tulang* dish. With a mob of pedestrians walking so briskly, I missed a step and twisted my ankle.

I was down flat on the floor. With the crowd continuing to walk briskly and no one offering to help me get up. One lady actually asked me to move out of the way. I was in great pain and mustered my strength to get up and hobble to the nearest chair I could find. There was a pawnshop a few meters away. I then asked in broken English. "Can sit down? Pain!" I said pointing to my foot. They let me sit for a few minutes.

But the serious foodie in me was not going to give up so easily. I was so close to the Golden Mile! I continued to the food center. There, I found several vendors selling this vibrant red dish. I chose to buy from the *mamak* (Indian hawker) stall with the most newspaper articles complimenting his *tulang*. The fierce-looking Indian vendor handed me a plate full of mutton bones glazed with this fire engine red sauce. I ordered a glass of lime juice to cool me down, and asked for a bag of ice to put on my now swelling ankle. I ate the *tulang* with my right hand while holding the ice over my left ankle. "What was I thinking," I thought to myself. The soup *tulang* was very unhealthy. And sipping the bone marrow coupled with the pain of the sprain, the title of the experience came to my head—"Killing Me Softly". For many weeks after that, I walked around with an ankle brace and had to wear my orange Nike running shoes all the time. It was definitely a fashion statement that did not sit well with many Singaporeans I encountered.

05

The Honeymoon is Over

Migrating to a new place stirs within the expatriate a roller coaster of emotions. Oftentimes it begins with either intense feelings of loving or hating the place.

Like most expats, I immediately fell in love with how easy living in Singapore is. They call it Asia Lite, Asia 101 or Asia for Beginners. Whatever the name, it is definitely a great first foreign posting for Westerners. But even for Asians like myself, the shift to Singapore is a breeze. It is such a contrast to the realities in my developing home country, the Philippines. I marvel at how everything is systematic. Filing for taxes, immigration requirements and other matters can be done online. I am comfortable taking the MRT, taxis, and buses without worrying about my safety. In Manila, I would drive myself in my van. Should I need to take a cab, I would send a friend or a family member a text message telling them the number plate of the cab I was riding in. In the event I was kidnapped or disappeared, they could then hopefully trace my whereabouts. But here it is different. Even if I go home close to midnight, I feel safe. I feel at ease walking alone, listening to my MP3 player and singing to my heart's content.

I do not have to look behind my shoulder to see if there is someone following me. If I want to go for a run or a walk at 3 or 4 in the morning, I can safely do so without worrying about my safety.

At first, I had a habit that drove my flatmate crazy. I would double lock the doors, fearing someone would break in late at night. I worried about our safety, since we were two single girls living in a condominium. But as I quickly realized my fears were unfounded, I came to peace with locking just the wooden door and keeping the grills unlocked all the time. I knew a European guy who would just leave his doors of his rented condominium unit unlocked day and night, even when he left for work, or went to bed. He never feared for his safety, or worried that anyone would steal anything. And in his six-month stay, nothing was ever stolen nor did he have any trespasser.

After three months in Singapore, with frequent trips back to Manila, I was settled in Singapore. I was hired to be an editor for one of the magazines with a local publishing company. I had met a Belgian expat, who arrived about the same time I had arrived in Singapore, and we started dating. I made good friends, some expats and some Filipinos. I found a community in a choir, comprised of Filipinos and one Singaporean. Together, we would sing twice a month at Church of St. Ignatius at King's Road. I had a life.

But once I started working at the publishing company, the honeymoon period in Singapore was soon over. My office was a large building near Geylang. It was not easily accessible by MRT, and for an artist who sought all things beautiful, it was sadly in an industrial area surrounded by many blah-looking warehouses. There were no pretty cafes or restaurants close to my office. The office itself often reminded me of a cold antiseptic hospital. Cold was actually an understatement. While Singapore's temperature often does not deviate far from 30°C, apparently there seems to be an evil conspiracy to create offices that mimic freezing Siberian winters. I quickly learned that a jacket was necessary, but there were some days I wish I had gloves and a muffler as well.

I am not only a morning person, but I also have a bright and sunny disposition to life. The words cheerful and friendly are not enough to capture my animated and warmth personality. Perhaps to many I am tad bit too quirky. And the shift to an office setting in Singapore was drastic for my free spirit. The mood was somber and very serious. My editorial team was even separated from the other magazine employees, with a glass partition, making me feel like I worked in a fish tank. I knew it was a prestigious travel title I was working for, but I did not realize how much stress came with working on this title. The stress was palpable within the confines of the fish tank. But most distinct was the deafening silence. I come from a culture of very chatty, expressive, and melodic people who sing at the drop of hat. In this office, conversation was minimal, in fact close to none. I felt awkward with the silence. I could almost hear myself breathe. With no other noise in the room, everyone could hear every single phone conversation.

I was so shocked by the silence. After several days, I finally asked my boss, "Is it really this quiet in offices in Singapore?" Then she humorously answered, "That's why we hired you." She later articulated that perhaps my sunny personality would ease the stress and tension within the fish tank. However the silence was so unnatural that I was not comfortable being my cheerful self. But there were short fleeting moments when I allowed myself to be natural and act as I normally would. I would then laugh and sing. To a colleague Cindy,

I would sing a commercial jingle of a fast food store of the same name. "When you're hungry, hungry, hungry, Cindy's is the place to be…" I'm not sure she was amused.

There was a canteen in our building with two concessionaires: a Muslim food vendor and a Chinese food vendor. I was faced with local fare every single day. While I tried eating breakfast as locals do, sampling *mee rebus* (a Malay egg noodle dish topped with a thick, sweet curry gravy, hard-boiled egg, tofu, chili, and bean sprouts), it was too heavy for my stomach so early in the day. I opted for apple celery juice and a grilled corned beef sandwich instead. With the huge amount of work, eating out was not a norm. In my first few weeks, I ate at my desk almost every single day. My editor and sub-editor would sit in their tables during lunch, continuing to work. I took the cue from them, and asked the graphic designers to buy our meals when they ate out. But after a few weeks, I verbalized my sadness in not going out for lunch to at least grab a quick bite, breathe some fresh air, and get some sunlight. My boss was startled that I was tired of the canteen options so soon.

There was a distinct office culture. Everyone had mugs with lids on them, perhaps to keep their beverage warm in the winter cold A/C. I amused myself with my stash of healthy snacks for our long hours, bringing in small Thai cucumbers, tomato juice, and tubs of yogurt. All of my colleagues perceived my eating habits as odd.

During the deadline season, when the magazine closed, I was eating breakfast, lunch and dinner in the office. It meant going home close to midnight, or even at 2:30 in the morning. And with my brain and body already weary, I still had to contend with cab drivers engaging in the now old conversation of "Where you from?" And telling them I am a Filipino, they would then go on asking,

"How long you in Singapore?" The others would try to charm me with Tagalog words, which was no longer amusing at two in the morning. Many would be curious, asking what work I was doing, and almost fascinated that I was both a Filipina and a working professional, as if that were unheard of. They would ask, "You single?" "Yes!" I would answer. "You have boyfriend?" "Yes." I would answer, hoping that would end their probing. Then as we drove up to my condominium, one cab driver said, "So, your boyfriend pay for your condo?" I was offended, but there was no point in answering this judgmental cab driver.

I lamented to my Indian colleague about my cab driver woes. She suggested that I should just plug in my iPod or pretend to be talking to someone on the phone, that way the cab driver would not talk to me. I thought it was just because I was Filipina. I was thinking of saying that I was from a different place, a country they were not familiar with. Maybe if I said I was from the Christmas Islands, I no longer had to deal with their stereotypes.

My weekday routine entailed getting squished in the packed MRT along with the rest of the workforce during the morning rush hour. I had to wake up early enough to make it before 8:15 for the company bus pick up at the Toa Payoh MRT station. In the evening, the company bus left three times at 6 pm, 6:15 pm and 6:30 pm. I often left the office later than this, requiring me to take the long voyage home on foot, on bus, on a crowded MRT, and then on foot again until I finally arrived home, one hour later. When I left work really late, it was the cab ride with the lengthy conversations I had to contend with.

By the time the weekend arrived, I was weary from the work week, preferring to just sleep in. There was a sad emptiness within me, a void I kept trying to fill but somehow kept failing. I am not the usual type of woman who loves shopping. But during this phase in my life, I found myself shopping. Not in a desire to look great, but just retail therapy to ease the emptiness.

My flatmate took advantage of every single holiday to go on trips to nearby Southeast Asian countries to dive or visit friends. And every time she went on a holiday, she left me to care for our plants. On one of these occasions, with my long hours at work, I had forgotten to water the beloved greens. So on Saturday I got up bright and early, with my head still somewhere in dreamland, I watered the plants on the balcony. Still groggy, I filled the pitcher with water and poured it out to every single pot. But my mind was not yet awake and I missed the pot and the water spilled to our neighbor's awning two floors below. I went about my business, taking a shower, getting ready to attend to all the weekend errands. After a while, I heard a knocking on my door. It was the security guard informing me of a formal complaint by the neighbor due to the water that was spilled. I explained I was just watering the plants and then headed down to the neighbor's home to apologize. The lady of the house was a Chinese lady. I apologized profusely. Then she said, "I thought it must have been a maid throwing dirty water down. Imagine, what if you got my husband wet. And our clothes got wet." I apologized again. I assured her it was not a delinquent maid, nor was it a malicious act. It was just an accident that happened. And I told her the water was definitely clean. Still very much upset, my apology was not received. I walked away, now upset at how such a minor incident became such a big deal. Had it happened to me, I would have let it slide. Had it happened with my neighbors in Australia and in the US, it probably wouldn't have caused such a stir.

In the past, I wondered why Singaporeans riding the MRT didn't smile a whole lot. Then, as I was going through this period in my life, I realized how tough life was for them. There was no life outside of work. I barely saw the sun or anything beautiful. I spent most of my waking hours in front of the computer, and I was not making meaningful relationships. I was not connecting with people. My official title was a Travel and Lifestyle Editor, but glued to my desk, I had no travel experiences, nor a good lifestyle to write about. I too had become miserable, just like those unsmiling MRT commuters.

I became so immersed in the Singapore lifestyle. My life became routine. And I was getting sick, with red blotches, an allergy perhaps from the stress. Noticing my very long hours and the many days of going home very late, my boyfriend finally jokingly said, "Are you sure you work for a magazine? Or do you really work in Geylang?" I answered back, "I don't think I even get paid enough. Perhaps the working girls in Geylang earn more."

After a series of late nights, it was past midnight when I headed to the ladies room to freshen up. As I washed my hands and caught a glimpse of my face in the mirror, looking back at me was a face I did not recognize. I had big black circles around my eyes just like a panda bear. But more frightening was the empty look in my eyes. I had never really prided myself on being a beautiful girl, but one thing I always had was the sparkle in my eyes. The reflection starting back at me definitely did not have that sparkle. And at the point, I realized it was not worth losing the spark in my soul for a job and a lifestyle I obviously did not enjoy.

Suddenly, everything just seemed cold and unfriendly. A woman I had accidentally touched in the MRT growled back at me. I felt her words to be harsh. I was used to people saying hello when you pass them on the street, or making small talk in the grocery shops or even in the bus or train. There was none of that here. When I did say hello and good morning to an older gentleman whom I crossed paths with every morning as I went for a walk, he was thrown off and avoided my eyes when our paths crossed again. Tears welled in my eyes in the MRT that day. I eventually told my flatmate of the story and she said she too missed the warmth of people saying hello as they did in her home, a small friendly town in Texas.

06 *Losing the Spark and Finding It All Over Again*

Losing the spark brought me into a process of finding myself all over again. Bit by bit, facets of who I was were stripped away. I ended my stint with the magazine and set up my own company to provide writing services for magazines and other publications. The whirlwind relationship I had with the romantic Belgian quickly crumbled when he was promoted and moved to China. Singapore was his first time living outside of his small town in Belgium. The ease and efficiency suited him. But when he moved to Wuxi, a city two hours away from Shanghai, the change was too drastic and too difficult. Seeing he was a foreigner who didn't speak English, a restaurant charged him equivalent to SGD $200 instead of the $30 listed in the menu for his meal. His colleagues were involved in shady business deals. And getting Internet service installed in his home was like a tooth extraction. Even having basic utilities sorted like heat and gas took a long time. None of this would have happened in Singapore.

I was left with the opportunity to recreate the life I wanted in Singapore. It was like I had a blank canvas to start my life anew. Thankfully, I had a network of supportive friends who took good care of me. These are real friends who are there in your lowest moments. They will take you out to First Thai, a quaint and authentic Thai restaurant in one of the shophouses at Purvis street for a comforting meal the day after the break-up. There's the other friend who spends hours with you walking up the Tree Top Walk and all around MacRitchie Reservoir, talking about each other's lives. The same friend provides the much-needed listening ear as you cry your heart out at a small park in Bishan. Then when the tears stop, together you indulge in a hearty dinner at Five Star Chicken Rice. There too is the friend who at a moment's notice takes the next bus and MRT from her office into the city to talk to you and buy you Ben & Jerry's ice cream at Raffles City Mall. She gently assures you everything will be ok.

Choosing to work solo again, I was now faced with many hours in a quiet condominium, unlike the home environment I was accustomed to in Manila where houses are always bustling with activity. There large families live together. There are always domestic helpers, drivers, and gardeners around, as well as friends and relatives constantly stopping by, and even pets cheering you up. In the Philippines, one is never really alone.

Life has a natural way of unfolding itself. Little by little, I found my comfort zones in Singapore. I poured my energies into making a go of my career as a food and travel writer, contributing to several magazines.

I soon discovered a solution to the loneliness and isolation of working alone from home. I found a Starbucks I felt comfortable to spend hours writing while drinking copious amounts of coffee. Then I found myself discovering pockets of Singapore that spoke to me. I discovered places which were cheerful and warm and friendly.

Joy, an architect friend, introduced me to the colourful world of Arab Street filled with shisha bars, fabric stores, and carpets from the Middle East. She used to work close to this area and whenever she needed a boost to her spirits, she would spend her lunch hour just popping in and out of the little shops here. There I met a Peranakan man who painstakingly continued the art of making beaded slippers. He happily welcomed us into his store, showing us finely beaded slippers costing several hundred dollars and other precious antiques he had collected. A very jovial entrepreneur Mr. Kim, who specialized in lacquer art pieces produced in Vietnam, was always delighted to see Joy and to engage his customers in long conversations on his latest creations.

Getting claustrophobic with the huge crowds in Orchard on a Sunday, my friend Chiquit and I discovered places like Portsdown Road. There, you can have a relaxing afternoon partaking of a chocolate tart and coffee, followed by a leisurely walk through streets with old colonial houses.

To stay connected with my faith and my culture, I joined the choir. That's one perk of moving to a foreign country, you get to reinvent your self and try new things you've never done before. Singing in a choir was a brand new experience for me. But beyond the singing, there was the camaraderie after mass. We would head off to Jologs on Lucky Plaza for our fix of Filipino food like *tapsilog* (beef slice with fried egg and garlic rice), *kare-kare* (peanut stew of ox tail with vegetables), and crispy *pata* (deep fried pork knuckles).

Yearning for green wide-open spaces and a feel of the countryside, I discovered the farms of Kranji. It is not exactly the rice paddies I had grown up seeing in the provinces of the Philippines or the mango orchard of my childhood summers, but there is a novelty to the farms here. I have never experienced seeing so many bullfrogs and the eerie sound of hundreds of them croaking in unison. It is fascinating to see young Singaporean city dwellers thrilled to see a goat for the first time and shrieking in delight as they feed them. Poison Ivy Bistro at Bollywood Organic Farm is refreshing. How wonderful it is to eat in an unmanicured setting, instead of perfectly decorated restaurants in the city.

Friday evenings offer many options. For affordable beers and a laid-back environment, there is Prince of Wales in Little India. This Aussie pub and backpacker hotel has a live band playing and even has a soft spot for international schoolteachers, giving them a discount on their booze. Or when I was seeking spiritual enlightenment, there was an affordable mediation class offered for three-consecutive Fridays at the Kadampa Meditation Center. The teacher Kelsang Chowang is an extremely cheerful Buddhist nun. When you meet her, she instantly makes you want to meditate, to have the same positive energy she exudes.

This island girl frequently needs a fix of the sun, sand, and the sea. I must admit the beaches pale miserably compared to the ones of the Philippines. The large shipping vessels don't really make the waters inviting for a swim. But just the same heading to a beach is still fun. Sentosa is a favorite for many on a Sunday afternoon. For a wholesome family ambiance, there's a pizza lunch at Coastes, or an afternoon of people watching while the sun sets at KM8. There's an easy, breezy vibe at East Coast, with kids learning to bike or roller blade and family enjoying barbecues. Despite the plethora of tents pitched by the beachfront, I still manage to find some quiet spots away from the maddening crowd. A first date instantly turned romantic when the guy took me on a tandem bike ride to an idyllic secluded portion of the beach, perfect for intimate conversation and sneaking in a first kiss.

Katong, where the old rich of Singapore used to have vacation homes by the sea, remains a setting for Peranakan and Eurasian culture and cuisine. The pastel-colored shophouses and the friendly neighborhood ambiance reminds me of wandering the streets of Malacca in Malaysia. A trip to Pulau Ubin brings back memories of the remote provinces in the Philippines. Here, the kampung village life is still alive. And with only a hundred residents and no tall buildings, you feel like you have been transported many decades back into the past.

One great asset of Singapore is how accessible it is to its Asian neighbors. It is a central travel hub with many flights all over the world. Thanks to budget airlines, it is easy to head off to many Southeast Asian cities. Many friends flying to other destinations like Australia and India have stopovers in Singapore. They often opt to spend the night in this charming city, giving us time to catch and reconnect. Being so central and connected, I never feel isolated from family and friends. In fact, I even see some jet-setting friends more often in Singapore than I had in Manila.

More importantly, I learn that I enjoy my new home most when I travel. The airport is fabulous, my Australian friend who visited jokingly said she would be willing to travel to Singapore even just to eat and shop in Changi Airport. Being based in Singapore provides me with opportunities to travel to Malacca, Bangkok, back to Manila and the beaches of the Philippines, and even experience the luxury train from Bangkok to Singapore on The Eastern and Oriental Express.

And when I come back to Singapore, I find myself sighing happily to return to the ease of life in my newly adopted home.

Being Filipino in Singapore

In Singapore, there is a peculiar fascination with identifying your race. Government forms, bank applications, and the standard employment records of companies require you to indicate whether you are Chinese, Indian, Caucasian, or Malay. I shared with two other Filipino writers about my predicament as I didn't know which to indicate for I am neither one of these. Filipinos are fusion at its best, a mix of Chinese, Malay, and Spanish ancestry. One of them suggested I should tick the box for Other, then write on the blank: Amazing. I burst into laughter. Brilliant idea, after all the Filipinos indeed are an amazing race.

With the plethora of Overseas Filipino Workers all over the world, I always find a fellow Filipino anywhere I go. But I was not prepared for the sheer number and presence of Filipinos in Singapore.

In 1994, when I was studying in Australia, I had my first encounter with Singaporeans at the University of Western Australia. There was the Flor Contemplacion case, a controversial case ending in the execution of the Filipino maid. To many Singaporeans then, Filipino women were instantly associated as maids. A Singaporean in my dorm in Australia even told me boldly, "You know, you're the first Filipino I'm taking to who's my equal." I was not sure whether I was supposed to thank her, or act offended. It was true after all that there are a number of Filipinos working in Singapore as maids.

But not all Filipinos are maids. Undoubtedly, it is impossible to ignore the overpowering presence of Filipino domestic helpers congregating around Lucky Plaza along Orchard on a Sunday, with some pouring out to nearby parks near orchard, even some having a picnic and jamming with guitars in the Botanic Gardens. Not a day goes by that I don't hear Tagalog, our national language, spoken in the MRT or on the streets of Singapore.

But apart from being maids, cab drivers and other Filipinos tell me the travails of Filipino women working in Singapore. A cab driver warned me not to go to Little India on Sunday for Bangladeshi construction men are there looking for Filipino girlfriends. Another cab driver told me of how he dropped off a Bangladeshi man at a large home in a posh part of Singapore. A Filipino girl opened the back door, for she entertained men while her bosses were away. I wondered why many women arrived in the Cathedral dressed in revealing outfits, inappropriate for church. A friend then told me that these women had lucrative careers. After church, they worked as prostitutes. She looked at the bright side, at least they prayed first. It is also common for a maid to offer cleaning services on Sundays, their day off. Marissa, who was having an affair with the security guard of our condominium, came to clean my flatmate's room once a month. She told me how her previous Chinese employer's kids would hit and hurt her. She hardly had days off, too. But her Korean employer now treats here with kindness, and gives her Sundays off. But she tells me that yes, some Filipinas she knows have Singaporean boyfriends just to get money or expensive gifts.

The poverty in the Philippines, prompting these women to take such desperate measures, is depressing. But living in this society with such an impression of Filipino women, I am often faced with the daily challenge of people looking at me as a Filipino woman beyond the stereotype.

But it is not all grim. Having a large population of Filipinos also makes Singapore feel pleasantly familiar for me. I soon realize it comes with perks too.

One of the country's largest exports is our nurses. When my friend fell into a ditch while jogging at night, she was in pain with a broken hip. I brought her to Tan Tock Seng Hospital. At the ER was a nurse. She asked me if I was Filipino, and when I answered yes, she immediately gave us superior service. She quickly carried my friend out of the cab into a wheelchair, then put her ahead of the other patients on the list.

Shopping in a Mango boutique, the Filipino cashier realized I was Filipino. She generously swiped her employee card, meriting a 10 percent discount on my purchases. Buying a present for a friend in a home store, the sales clerk that attended to me was a Filipino. When he found out I too was Filipino, he didn't charge me for the giftwrapping service. Even the IKEA customer service phone attendant promised to give me free screws to repair my bed frame if I went all the way to the Tampines branch. On another occasion, a waiter happily gave my visiting father an extra generous serving of soup for he was Filipino.

There is a strong bond that unites us. Perhaps the joy and familiarity of encountering a fellowman eases the homesickness of being away from home. I call it my Filipino mafia, a strong network of kindness you can rely on, anywhere in the world.

Despite the poverty and difficulty, truly we are resilient people. And next time someone asks me my race, I will boldly tell them I belong to this amazing race.

07 *Everyday Singapore*

After the seventh or eighth month, the novelty of living in Singapore wanes. And it becomes a natural way of life. The ease and efficiency of life becomes part and parcel of your own life, and Singapore's own distinct everyday culture unfolds before you.

Mrt and Buses

The MRT provides me with a microscopic view of Singaporean society. Truly, it is a convenient and affordable transport system that gets you around Singapore fast. I learned the hard way that it is definitely unacceptable to attempt to bring a suitcase during the morning rush hour from 7:30 am till about 9:30 am when the trains are packed. You will get hostile stares from fellow passengers.

Everything happens in the MRT, and there is never a dull moment. For some reason, Singaporeans always seem to have to keep themselves busy and stimulated. Kids and grown adults in suits are constantly playing games on their playstations, mobile phones, and even laptops on the train. Some watch movies on portable TVs. And it is not uncommon to see mothers fight with their kids so they can play the games. Having an iPod or MP3 player is an essential everyday gadget to survive commuting in Singapore. I quickly learned that music makes time go by faster. They are especially handy in distracting you from the very packed train rides or long walks home. I've discovered audio books as a great way to spend your travel time on the MRT.

On other occasions, I amuse myself people watching. I was disgusted to see a mom cut not just her own fingernails in the train, but to proceed to cut her children's nails too. There are the annoying people who talk loudly throughout the duration of their train ride. One person I met told me how annoyed she was with a Chinese lady who stepped on her shoes while talking loudly on her mobile phone. The now irate passenger called the attention of the insensitive woman, but she continued talking on the phone, thinking the woman did not understand Chinese. Now fuming mad, the passenger grabbed the woman's phone and threw it out of the MRT door when it opened at the next stop. Very early one morning, I was in the train when a man stared at the guy across him. He said out loud, "Hello! Hello! How much your shoes?" I was so surprised at his boldness. But the other guy gave the exact price and where he got it. A doctor friend studying to be a cardio-thoraxic surgeon finds the MRT and buses the most conducive place for studying. He simply boards the MRT and sits there studying until he reaches the end of the line. If he gets hungry, he hops off the train, gets some food, and hops back on to study again.

There are certain seats on the train marked for passengers with special needs like the elderly, pregnant women, or little children. I often find myself giving my seat to the elderly who struggle to keep their balance on the train. But I notice that it is consistently the women who offer their seats, while the men sit comfortably unaffected by the whole situation. Is chivalry dead in Singapore? But at the same time, I am baffled why Singaporean men feel comfortable carrying their girlfriends' handbags. Is that their attempt at being gentlemanly?

The bus system in Singapore is commendable. I marvel at how synchronized the buses are. If you are waiting for a bus, and you see the bus number stop in the bus stop across you, you can be certain your bus will soon be on its way.

On Shopping

There is no doubt shopping is a way of life in Singapore. Weekends are synonymous with shopping. And malls often stay open till ten in the evening. Many women linger at the malls after work to lust over the latest bag or shoes they fancy. I have never been in a country where grocery shopping can be so stressful. Close to my home is a Fair Price at Ang Mo Kio hub. It is more than a grocery store, it also sells appliances, bed sheets and clothes. It is almost like a Target store in the US. But with the store so crowded on weekends, you actually experience bumper-to-bumper grocery carts. It gets even more stressful when the kids who are tasked to push the grocery carts are distracted by the games on their playstations.

On Singlish

While a multi-cultural society yields a rich culinary experience in Singapore, it has not resulted positively on the language. Singlish is the English-based Creole spoken widely. "Lah" is sneaked in at the end of phrases and sentences. But it is actually more complex than that. It often sounds like very bad choppy English, without prepositions.

After a while you find yourself shortening your conversations, saying "can" instead of "I can do it". And for some reason, you catch on and say "Is it?" as well. "Auntie" and "Uncle" are often used, even if you are not related to the older person. The government has a Speak Good English Movement in place, aggressively promoting better use of the language. But sometimes, there's no choice but to use Singlish to be understood, lah!

How Efficient is Efficient?

Singaporeans have elevated efficiency into an art form. While many countries have a fast lane and a slow lane on the highways, the escalators in Singapore have the same system. People who are not in a rush must stand on the left, while those who want to get ahead can manually walk up the escalator on the right. Standing on the right lane is definitely taboo, for you are delaying the fast ones from getting ahead.

I can be absent-minded at times. In my rush to top up my EZ-Link card, an automated card stored with cash for use in the MRT and buses, I did not wait for the light to turn green, so my $10 top up was not credited to my card. I told the attendant in the station of my little problem. He filed the report, and in less than two weeks I got a refund in the mail.

But in getting used to the efficiency and the safety of living in Singapore, we let our guard down. We become complacent and leave our laptops unattended in cafes while we run to the restroom. Wanting to buy some dinner home after some grocery shopping, I left my groceries unattended for a few minutes, only to return to find some bags missing. The thief was obviously a connoisseur, leaving my veggies and pork behind. But the discriminating eater took off with my packs of fine Ghiradelli chocolate and other pricey groceries.

A Journal Entry,
17 Sept 2007: Sharing a Table in Singapore

I moved to Singapore three weeks ago. I settled quickly into a lovely apartment in Yio Chu Kang which I share with an American schoolteacher in a record time of three days. I have fallen in love with the ease and efficiency of the MRT, and have even memorized the stops on the red line. But, I am still adjusting to the food culture. I must admit my Filipino tongue is not accustomed to spicy food. The intense chili flavor of many hawker dishes are beyond the tolerance of my extremely sensitive taste buds. I'm also shocked that people buy cooked food rather than cook their meals. But then it starts to make sense to me. If you can eat a full meal with meat, vegetables, and rice for as low as $2.20, why would you go through all the trouble of cooking and cleaning up? Aside from the flavor and the prevalence of hawker stores everywhere, the concept of sharing a table is still new to me.

In the Philippines, there is so much space. It is rare to share a table with total strangers. Plus, Filipinos tend to be very private. Our actions are governed by *hiya*. It loosely translates to being shy or modest. But more importantly, it is the fear of losing face or this intense desire to please or conform to the expectation of the bigger group. Sharing a table can be *nakakahiya*, for you are intruding into the affairs of other people.

One of my daily rituals as a writer is the luxury of sipping a cup of cappuccino in an air-conditioned coffee shop. I linger for hours, nursing not just my caffeine beverage but also my thoughts for an article. In my new place in Singapore, I have yet to find a coffee house to linger. After some research, I learned I could walk 15 minutes to the MRT, hop on for two stops to Yishun and find a Starbucks there. But it isn't cheap, considering a cup of coffee in Starbucks costs more than the price of dining hawker style.

But desperately missing my afternoon café luxury, I headed to Ang Mo Kio Hub. There I found Ah Mei, a charming local café serving *teh tarik*, *kopi*, and a selection of *roti prata*, *kaya* toast, and *briyani*. With one hand holding my cuppa and the other balancing the plate of *roti prata* and curry, I could not find a seat. I asked in English if I could share a table with a couple. But as they did not speak much English, it became a confusing exchange of words. I later learned they were saving it for their companion. Empty seat after empty seat was reserved. And one of rejection after another felt rather harsh.

Finally, I spotted two empty seats next to a middle-aged couple. They kindly moved aside the dirty plates next to them to make room for me. I realized the place was very busy. It would be an extremely inconsiderate act to sit and linger for hours with my thoughts. Hence, I quickly ate my *prata*. Feeling rather vulnerable and awkward, I stared into space. I heard the woman tell her husband how the chicken was rather dry, and next time they should eat the fish instead. They then got up in search of a post office.

Lost in thought and dissatisfied, I wondered if there was a coffee shop nearby where I could sit for hours. I then sipped my *teh tarik*, and a new set of diners came to eat. They were thrilled to find three empty seats next to me. I sat oblivious to their company, or at least pretending to be.

They were a group of three pairs of husband and wives, all probably in their sixties. One man was certain he wanted some *prata*. It seemed like they already had lunch although it was only two in the afternoon. The woman sitting next to me lamented to another woman how her husband shouldn't eat too much. She was just having *kopi*. When the *prata* arrived along with cups of *kopi* and tea, the woman continued saying how much better it was to eat *prata* at home—it was crisp and not only when toasted in the oven.

The man across me happily enjoyed his *prata* and announced he wanted a place like this close to his house. The proximity of my dining companions felt awkward. I desperately wanted to chime in their conversation, but I didn't want to be rude.

Until finally, I broke my silence and asked where I could get this frozen *prata*. She told me to get it in the supermarket. "What about good curry to dip it in?" Interestingly, everyone joined in the conversation. When they found out I was a food writer, they gave me their suggested places to eat. From the best *prata* to the best fish head curry to the best chicken rice to the best ice cream, these food-loving Singaporeans had a recommendation for me.

All the earlier feelings of rejection quickly vanished. I felt right at home with them. We did not exchange names. But I gave them my business card. The conversation must have lasted for about 30 minutes, definitely much longer than it took me to eat my *prata* and drink my tea. They even drew maps in my notebook and wrote in Chinese words which I could easily show the cab driver to guide me on my food scavenger hunt.

They told me they spend afternoons together. They appeared to be retired, but seemed youthful. And when the talk on ice cream lingered, the woman sitting next to me lamented how she had not yet tasted the ice cream from Island Creamery. David, the leader of the pack, told me about how the ice cream was better and cheaper than Haagen Daz. And the flavors were truly different, from Tiger Beer to Horlicks. He was impressed when I showed him a photo in my digital camera, recounting my experience of having tasted it hours upon my arrival in Singapore.

The talk on ice cream was too enticing, they decided to head to Island Creamery right that very moment. They even invited me to go with them. I begged off, thinking of all the work I should be doing. They then said that if I ever needed companions to eat with, just give them a call, and they would gladly accompany me or even drive me to the place.

I've read a sign somewhere enticing its diners to share a table. The sign read, "Share a table, gain a friend." I guess I could get used to this Singaporean eating custom. Perhaps I will adapt to it faster than my taste buds can adjust to the spicy chilis.

08

The Good, the Bad and the Ugly

Of the 4.68 million population of Singapore in mid-2007, the expatriate population constitutes 24 percent of this figure. Concentrated in one small island, it is a presence that cannot be ignored.

Mention the word expat and the image of a high-powered Caucasian businessman comes to the minds of many. The word *ang moh* originates from the Hokkien reference of white people in Singapore. But Singapore's expats are not just *ang mohs*, neither are they just the usual businessmen in suits. It is a growing eclectic mix of individuals coming from everywhere. Despite its small population, it is blessed with a diverse mix of people. Living in this country, I've met people from everywhere: Zimbabwe, South Africa, Australia, New Zealand, Italy, France, US, Canada, Japan, Germany, Belgium, and Egypt. It is a mini-global village.

Indeed, living anywhere comes with the good, the bad, and the ugly. Having a gift for making friends at the drop of a hat, I easily meet interesting people here. That is one of the best assets of Singapore—it attracts a colorful expat population. As I negotiate living in Singapore, my life somehow lends itself to meeting fascinating expatriates from diverse and varied backgrounds. The Lion City provides the backdrop to our relationships, but being expatriates is also the glue that binds us together. We are bound together by the shared experience of living in Singapore.

As my life unfolds in my new home, I revel in meeting global citizens like myself who have lived in many countries. I rejoice in encountering people who share my passions for travel and cultures. Like me, these people are comfortable in establishing and re-establishing a home over and over again in different parts of the world. I marvel at how friendships are easily forged beyond race, religion or culture. I am overjoyed when we deeply connect. Instead of focusing on our differences, we joyfully celebrate what we share.

It is said that the world is getting smaller. There is the famous idea that there is six degrees of separation in this world, that if a person is one step away from each person they know and two steps away from each person who is known by one of the people they know, then everyone is at most six steps away from any other person on Earth.But in Singapore where the population is small within a compact island, the six degrees of separation perhaps becomes even smaller. Many have told me that it is two degrees of separation here.

As the days pass by and I go on living my life in Singapore, my life shifts from just knowing the nuns and a handful of people in the magazine world to developing a very international network of people. We share the experience of living in this island. Coming from the US, the Philippines, Italy, France, Germany, Australia, New Zealand, Japan, Thailand and India, and with varied backgrounds from teachers to baristas, artists, meditation teachers, photographers and stay-at-home moms, each one tells me an interesting story. But more fascinating is how our lives have naturally connected.

As I tell you how we met and each one's story, I wish to share how rich my life has become by moving to Singapore. May you discover the good, the bad, and the ugly in Singapore as seen through the eyes of these strangers, who have become my friends.

As many people expect the stereotypical expat to be a Caucasian male working for a bank and living in a condominium in Holland Village, I've learned this does not hold true. The foreigners moving to Singapore are changing. And their varied cultures, eclectic backgrounds, and the lifestyles that they bring allow for a more diverse community to emerge in Singapore.

I believe everyone has a story to tell. In the next section of the book, the journey of people who were once strangers and now my friends will unfold. They have trusted me with their stories, generously sharing private details of their lives. Through these stories, may you get a glimpse of the real lives of expats as we journey through living in Singapore.

Part II

EVERYONE HAS A STORY TO TELL

09 *Coming into Focus*

Scott Woodward, Canadian
34 years old, Travel Photographer,
Moved to Singapore in June 1997, Married with no kids

How We Met

When I tell people I am a food and travel writer, almost instantly a dreamy look is cast on their faces. People have this notion that I constantly get whisked off to glamorous hotels and resorts, dine in the most expensive restaurants, and get the ultimate three-hour spa treatments. Let me burst the bubble and tell you the truth. The reality is that it rarely happens. Often, I am roughing it up in less than idyllic conditions.

No one can commiserate more than my friend, Scott Woodward, a travel photographer. Scott and I met in May 2007 when we were working on two stories for *Smile*, an in-flight travel magazine for a budget airline in the Philippines. I had mastered the art of traveling solo around my beloved archipelago. But I was worried when my editor told me she was sending a Canadian photographer to join me on my trip to Siargao, a fantastic surfing destination, located in the southern island of Mindanao. It is no secret that many foreigners have been kidnapped in the Mindanao. It was even more risky as it worked out that we would be traveling on Election Day, when there was more likelihood of violence. Add one more fact, there are more journalists killed in the southern portion of the Philippines.

Fearing he would be an instant target for kidnapping, I desperately asked my editor, "Is there some way he can look less Caucasian?" But they both remained unfazed, and the two of us proceeded with our two-destination assignment covering Siargao and a secluded island called Sugar Beach.

Traveling with a stranger for almost ten days in challenging conditions can bond you for life or turn into a living nightmare. Thankfully, Scott and I got along swimmingly well despite what we had to endure on this trip. His ordeal began in Manila when he was billeted in a dirty hotel in Chinatown. It was appalling. Scott showed me the bloodstains on the upholstery and the thick film of dust in his hotel room when I picked him up on our way to the airport. To complete our team, they sent a naïve 17-year-old model, instantly making us act as her responsible guardians. The journey to the surf destination alone took over 24 hours of riding a plane, a tricycle, a bus, a tricycle again, a ferry, a van, a motorcycle, and a stay in a shabby hotel.

And the true trooper that he was, this Canadian photographer only complained twice: when the conductor on the bus kept bumping his butt on Scott's face to collect tickets from other passengers and when the airport security repeatedly inquired about his tripod. Scott gamely rode on motorcycles with me and a local, slept on a bunk bed, waking up with his legs dotted with numerous mosquito bites, and even rode a rented van with goons instructing us to pretend to be a married couple should the police stop us at the checkpoint on the way to the airport.

On our second assignment at Sugar Beach, our schedule was more relaxed and we had no model to look after. We stayed in an extremely quirky cottage, decorated with installation art. It was odd to awake to a dangling mermaid mannequin over your head and coke cans used as bed frames. But Scott's big challenge happened when he was photographing a cute little kid on a tree swing by the beach. It was such an idyllic scene of rural life. She gently pushed off the swing as Scott snapped away. I told her in the local dialect that she was doing a good job, and to keep doing it. To our surprise, she poured all her energy into one big push. With the giant momentum, the next thing I knew her feet went veering right smack into Scott and his camera. Acting quickly, he was not hurt. He dodged straight into the sand, getting very fine particles of sand onto his precious lens. Naturally upset, he retreated to the resort. But in an hour or so, Scott and I were back on the beach, capturing the sweet island life at this destination.

After our long workdays, we would unwind and share life stories over bottles of San Miguel beer. At this point, I was almost sure it was time to leave the Philippines. I had ticked off all the destinations I wanted to cover in my archipelago. I wanted to live in a new place. Listening to Scott's stories, Singapore seemed to be a good bet. Add to the fact that most of my editors were based there too. Scott not only encouraged the move, he also offered his spare room should I need a place to stay when I got there.

Being one of the few friends I had in Singapore, I immediately looked him up when I arrived. His studio in Ann Siang Hill was one of the first places I learned to get to. Chinatown is a hub for people working in publishing with several PR firms, ad agencies, and magazines offices looking smart in the chic shophouses on Amoy Street alongside quaint restaurants, boutiques, and little artsy designer stores. Conveniently located close to my editor's office on Amoy Street, I would detour to his studio before heading to the Tanjong Pagar MRT.

Scott became my sounding board and wise adviser for my career as a freelance food and travel writer. If I found myself in the area with my spirits low, I would send a message asking if I could stop by. I would always get ribbing from him for being sweaty from my walk. I would then plop myself on his chair while he worked on his photos. We would catch up on lamentations and challenges of getting paid or finding new opportunities. We would balance it off by sharing little successes and dreams, like writing for *Saveur* and *Bon Appetit* for me, and getting his photos published in the *National Geographic*. It was also Scott's dazzling recommendation of me to the editor of Singapore Airlines' *Silver Kris* magazine that merited an introductory meeting, and eventually a job as a travel and lifestyle editor.

His Story

Instead of the usual 10-minute catch up on each other's lives, Scott and I finally made good on our promise to have lunch one sunny Friday. He chose his favourite steak house, Les Bouchons, a few steps away from his studio on Ann Siang Hill. Each with a hefty piece of meat and mountain of frites before us, this travel photographer narrated how his life came into focus in Singapore. When I asked him the very first time I met him in Manila how he became a travel photographer, he answered "I was just at the right place at the right time." Perhaps it is his polite, short answer for people who don't really know him or don't really care. But after truly getting to know this accomplished friend and colleague of mine, I realise it is not mere coincidence of timing and being in the right place. Rather, his story is a journey of adventure, growing up, maturing, and living his dreams—all these unfolding here in Singapore.

Meeting Scott for the first time, he comes across as a well-traveled, charming and eloquent urbanite. But this 34-year-old Canadian tells me he is a small town boy. He grew up in Fonthill, Ontario, a town of 8,000 people located close to the Niagara Falls. His family holidays were road trips or time spent at a cottage by the lake. But as fate had it, this small town boy's roommate in college was Jamie, a Canadian born in Winnepeg but who grew up in Hong Kong.

Describing his roommate, Scott tells me how different their backgrounds were, "Jamie's dad is an expat, so he was in Hong Kong since he was three or four and lived there all his life. So I heard all these amazing stories about Asia, which was awe-inspiring for me. He had all these photos of Nepal, Koh Samui, and all these wonderful experiences." In contrast, Scott then had only been on a plane once or twice in his life. He admits, "Asia was not even on my radar."

With his curiosity about Asia piqued, Scott decided to take a big adventure at the end of his first year in university: "My dad gave me a credit card for emergencies when I started university. I used it to buy an airplane ticket to visit Jamie and his mom and dad in Hong Kong. It was eye-opening. It is the world we live in now, but at that time it was so foreign, it made my head spin."

Living in Jamie's family's big apartment, riding a junk boat at the Hong Kong Harbour, and the thrill of Victoria's Peak made for the thrilling adventure of a lifetime for Scott. Not getting enough of his first trip to Asia and fun times with his best buddy, this young Canadian returned to visit Jamie after graduating from university. Jamie moved back to Asia. He was working in a Management Trainee Program for Coca-Cola in Vietnam. Scott visited his buddy, and spent the year backpacking in Vietnam, Malaysia, Indonesia, Australia, Singapore, and Thailand.

Halfway through his big immersion in the East, Scott met Jamie's boss in Coca-Cola, Mr. McKinney, who lived in Singapore. Mr. McKinney offered Scott a similar opportunity in Singapore, but there was still Indonesia and Australia to explore in the young traveler's itinerary. After finishing his extensive backpacking adventure, he returned back to Canada. He reconnected with Mr. McKinney and accepted the job in Singapore. He quickly packed his belongings and moved to Asia three weeks later.

As luck would have it, Coca-Cola relocated Jamie from Vietnam to Singapore. The college roommates decided to share an apartment. Scott happily recalls, "It was like university all over again, with money this time." They had gone a long way from the apartment they rented in Canada for $400/month to their four-bedroom condominium in Singapore at $4000/month.

Imagine the joy of having your best buddy and getting all the glorious perks of being an expat. Scott aptly calls themselves "Exbrats". The memory of the charmed life remains vivid in his mind. "I had this job where I was making very good money. I had tones of disposable income. It was an exciting time. Like wow, this is as good as it gets." The executives in Coca-Cola at the time had brand new BMWs. When they were traveling, Jamie and Scott had the privilege of driving them. They would go out to Emerald Hill,

Chijmes, and Zouk. Fresh out of college, these two bachelors had too much space in their four-bedroom house. Scott says, "We had one bedroom each, a spare room, and one room was just for our mountain bikes. It was good times." Young and naïve, the two guys thought they would work for the company forever. At 22, Scott thought he had it made, "It was the dream job, the perfect office, suit, and tie. It was great, you think you're king of the world. It was happy times." The only downside at the time was that his girlfriend Stacey was in Canada.

After a year or so, Scott's girlfriend paid him a visit. Stacey was then completing her teaching degree, which required her to do six weeks of practical teaching. She chose to do it in the Canadian International School in Singapore. When she completed it, the new Canadian teacher received a job offer from the Singapore American School in June 1998. She accepted the job, and is now in her eleventh year of teaching in the same school.

Along with the charmed life came responsibility. Just when his girlfriend was ready to settle down in Singapore, Scott was promoted to work in Coca-Cola's Marketing and Sales Department in Ho Chi Minh City in Vietnam. His girlfriend then took over his room, and shared the apartment with Jamie. It was a difficult time. But the young lovers remained connected and would take turns in visiting each other every few weeks in Vietnam or Singapore.

While Scott lived a pampered and luxurious life in Asia, it was not all fun and games. He explains, "It was challenging in the beginning because there were significant cultural differences. Asia respects age and wisdom and I was young and foreign. It was challenging to get their respect." It didn't help that being a young manager put Scott in an interesting position. "There were a lot of employees who were my dad's age, in their late 40s and 50s, and thinking, 'who's this young foreign kid?' That was a challenge!"

Through the training of his mentors, Scott quickly learned it was not about working hard, but working harder than his fellow employees. He tells me, "When I was in sales and marketing, I was going out in the truck with the guys, or loading the Coke myself. If you want the guys to be there at 7, you'd be there at 6.45. If you want the trucks loaded early, you help load them up."

Scott then returned to Singapore to at last be with Stacey in December 1999, finally living in their own condominium. When he finished his tenure with Coca-Cola, he then moved on to work with the agency of Coke, McCann Ericsson for one year. He later moved to DBS, working on the branding and advertising of the bank for a year until almost the entire group was made redundant. American Express took him on, where he worked for four years in the marketing group with numerous work trips around Asia.

But despite everything going well in his life, as Scott neared his 30th year, an unsettling feeling started to surface. A bit early to be his mid-life crisis, he calls it his "One-third life crisis". It was a feeling he could not shake off. He tries to articulate this phase in his life. "I was kinda feeling like where did my twenties go? I started to remember random little things, like what I wore to get my driver's license, etc. It was almost like this nostalgia thing was just over me. I wasn't unhappy but I wasn't overly thrilled. I can't really explain it. I was just having a hard time turning thirty. It felt like my 'childhood' was over. It was just really hard. It sounds silly."

This one-third life crisis was pervasive and could not be ignored. "In January 2004, I was starting to feel this way, almost a full year before my thirtieth year birthday. And I remember there was a Chinese

New Year dinner that Amex organized. Quite frankly I really didn't want to go. But I went anyway, being the good corporate citizen that I was." He recalls, "I was seated at a table with colleagues, some of whom I knew, and the rest of them I only knew in passing. Then someone in the table said, 'Let's play a game.' I was like 'oh a game, that's awesome, exactly what would make tonight better.' The game asked questions like, 'If you had one last day on earth, how would you spend it? If you had one last meal on earth, what would it be?' There were so many different nationalities, age groups, and genders in the table. Everyone was so different. The answers were quite intriguing. The American guy said he'd have the biggest steak he could find. The French guy said he would wake in the morning and start with …, describing his whole day of eating, even the places he would eat at. So it was just interesting to see the cultural differences."

"The final question was, 'If you had whatever your magic money number is, say 10 million dollars, or 100 million dollars, if you had enough money and did not have to worry about earning a living, what would you do tomorrow, and what would you do everyday thereafter that would bring you joy?' At that time, I was managing the marketing for the Platinum and Centurion cards for 13 countries in Asia. We handled Japan, Asia Pacific, Australia, and New Zealand. It was massive." Scott was surprised with his own answer to the bunch of people he did not really know very well. He said, "I'd travel around the world and take photographs."

He went home that night, wide awake for hours. With his wife sleeping next to him, he stared at the ceiling thinking, "If that's my answer to a bunch of strangers, what am I doing with my life?" He then made a promise to make photography a bigger part of his life, taking more photos not just on holidays, but also shooting around

Singapore. He also got to work on putting together a portfolio of his best hundred photos, and converted them from negatives to digital images with the help of his friend, Mike, a creative director from TBWA. He started showing his portfolio to creative people, artists, painters, and marketing people, landing him an offer to join a small arts and crafts exhibition in a woman's house. He got ten of his best photographs printed and framed, with the goal to sell just one photo to a stranger. He surpassed his expectations and sold 35 photos.

His confidence grew. While he continued working with American Express during the day, he devoted his nights and weekends to his love for photography. With his excellent marketing and sales background, he managed to build a brand and a name for himself as a photographer. While this was going on, his tumultuous time hitting thirty still persisted.

Despite his apprehension with his upcoming 30th birthday, his wife managed to convince him to have a party. His birthday was the day after Christmas. She arranged a champagne brunch at the Fullerton Hotel with 16 of his closest friends. He vividly remembers the significant day, "It was a wonderful day. We all got dressed up. The sun was coming through the window and it was really a beautiful day. It was fun. In the middle of brunch, I got a phone call from a very good friend of mine who worked in Amex with me. She was hysterical. She was at the tsunami at Phuket. I selfishly thought she called to send her birthday wishes. I had no idea. But I remember her calling and being hysterical, asking for help." With his connections in Amex handling the Centurion accounts, his friend figured Scott could assist in getting them out of Phuket during that emergency.

At that moment things gelled together for Scott, "Me, turning 30, kinda having that 'I don't know what to do with my life', this photography business that was burgeoning and this passion awakening inside me. This cataclysmic event sort of rammed home that nothing lasts forever. You've got to seize the day. So I quit my job."

That was only four years ago. But Scott has gone a long way from working at his dining room table at home to having his own studio in a hip shophouse at Ann Siang Hill in Chinatown. Just two months ago, I joined Stacey and Scott's closest friends to celebrate the realization of his big dream. *National Geographic* recently published a photo he shot in Bhutan of monks running down the hill. This hotshot photographer's client list includes impressive magazine titles like *The National Geographic*, *Travel & Leisure*, and the *New York Times*, plus brands like Adidas and Nokia rely on him to shoot their major print advertising campaigns.

Sitting across Scott as we dine alfresco at his favorite restaurant, Singapore's warm sunshine beams straight at this photographer. I listen to him narrate his story. The intense passion, dedication and commitment he has for his craft is tangible. He had just returned from a three-week trip shooting around Laos, Cambodia, and Vietnam for *Travel & Leisure* Australia Magazine. While he enjoys the adventure of travel photography, he cannot imagine living anywhere but Singapore. He confides, "Singapore is a great base. It's tax favorable for small business owners. It's got fantastic infrastructure, like high speed internet access I need for uploading huge volumes of files." In Cambodia, it took him three hours to upload three files. But he is not fazed by these problems in Singapore.

With much conviction, Scott boldly states his love for Singapore. "I can't imagine living anywhere else in Asia. I've been to many places and there are other cities that are absolutely exciting. I don't think I want to live in Hong Kong, Bangkok, Jakarta or Manila. These are fun places to visit. But this is my home." He echoes what others have said, "It's got the clichés everybody says. It's got an inexpensive public transit. Taxis are inexpensive and abundant. It's such a small place, making it easy for me to get to my client meetings."

He goes on listing other favorable factors in living here. "It's got a wonderful climate." But more importantly for his job, "It's got an efficient airport because I'm traveling a lot. So there are flights everywhere all the time. Singapore's a great hub." He sums it up, "From a practical point of view, it makes sense. From an emotional point of view, I love it here. It has become my home. Definitely for Stacey and I both. We feel comfortable here. We like it here. We've got a good network of friends here."

With Scott's ongoing love affair with Asia, his excellent marketing skills, and fantastic eye for photography, there is no doubt he will be one of the best photographers in the world. Surely his job will take him to countless countries, exploring several more with Stacey on their holidays. But there will only be one home, and it is Singapore. For it is right here in Singapore that Scott has gotten into clearer focus with his lifework, his passion, and his true love.

10

God Has A Wicked Sense Of Humor

Rachel*, Filipino
38 years old, Public Relations Professional, Permanent Resident,
Moved to Singapore on 14 January 1993, Single

How We Met

Moving to Singapore with the nuns as my first friends had many perks. Not only did they pray for me, they also looked after my spiritual well-being. Sr. Mel, a Filipino nun from the Religious of the Cenacle, invited me to join a bible study she conducted for a group of single Filipino professionals working here.

One month from my arrival, I found myself in the home of Joy, a Filipino architect who had been living in Singapore for many years. She lived in a new condominium unit just across the Bedok Reservoir. One of her clients owned the two-bedroom furnished unit and leased it to her for a bargain. And on this day, the bible study group was hosted in her home, doubling as a house blessing for her recent move into the unit. There, I met a merry mix of personalities of five women and one guy. With a spread of Filipino dishes on the table, it began with a hearty lunch and much bantering. It was loud and noisy, as it is when old friends have not seen one another in a long time. They welcomed me warmly, unsure really what to expect from a food and travel writer friend of the nun. If they expected a goody two shoes girl, none of them showed their disappointment in meeting me, a crazy, unconventional Catholic girl.

One person stood out from the group, a lady named Rachel. When she arrived, the group was shocked to see tight curls on her head. Obviously self-conscious of her new look, she made jokes about it. Rachel, it turned out, worked for Disney Channel's PR Department. She had a positive energy to her, and a refreshing confidence to make fun of herself. After studying some chapters in the bible, the group would share a personal reflection. Rachel had been lamenting to God about how ugly she looked with her newly permed hair. She would lift up her hair woes to God. After all, she said, two themes in her life rang true, "God really takes care of us and that God has a wicked sense of humor."

The bible study was held every month, either in a home of one of the members or in the Cenacle Retreat House in Jurong West. Rachel was instrumental in organizing schedules and making it happen. She and most members of the bible study group were also part of the Francis Xavier Choir, which sings twice a month in a Jesuit-run Catholic Church on Kings Road close to Holland Village. They encouraged me to join them and sing every second and fourth Sundays of the month.

It is often a stereotype that all Filipinos sing well. True, the performing comes naturally for Filipinos, be it a song, dance, acting, or even combining all three skills. But singing is almost innate, even just speaking in Tagalog sounds melodic to non-speakers. But in my family, performing a song or dance was not highly encouraged. While I could carry a tune, it never really occurred to me to join a choir. I didn't think my voice was superior to others.

When I moved to Singapore, I tried a new church each Sunday hoping to find the parish that suited me. I attended mass in the Cathedral of the Good Shepherd, and the churches in Ang Mo Kio, Toa Payoh, Novena, and at St. Peter and Paul in Bras Basah. Novena had a large population of mass-goers, overflowing outside the church. They've installed TV monitors for those who could not sit inside the church. In one mass, I participated in the Eucharist Celebration by actively singing. At the end of the mass, a Singaporean standing next to me asked, "Will you be here next week?" I told her I was not sure. She said, "I hope you would be back. I'd like to stand next to you. You sing very well."

Thrilled by her compliment, I took it as my cue to finally succumb to my bible study friends'—Agnes and Rachel—invitation to join the choir. So twice a month, dressed in a white blouse, we sang our hearts out on Saturday nights at St. Ignatius Church.

Behind her warm smile and bubbly personality, there was evidently a deep faith residing in Rachel's soul. In time, she became more than just a person I saw in bible study or choir. When she learned my Belgian boyfriend had broken up with me, she immediately took me out to dinner after work at Yum Cha in Chinatown to ease my aching heart. There were after choir dinners of Filipino home cuisine at Jologs in Lucky Plaza, and even dining at Chat Masala Too, one of her favorite Indian restaurants in Bukit Timah. When we were both in Manila last Christmas, we found ourselves joyfully bursting into laughter and nursing many glasses of wine in a common friend's lovely studio in the heart of Makati.

The more I got to know Rachel, the more I was certain she had a wonderful story waiting to burst out of her nicely caramel complexion. This private person was initially hesitant to share, but with some gentle coaxing, she agreed to narrate her story to me. So one Saturday afternoon, we agreed to meet in Cedele, tucked in the third floor of Raffles City. It is a challenge to find a quiet café in the heart of Singapore, where you can linger for hours unrushed and far from the maddening crowd. But close to the appointed time, a frazzled Rachel was panicking. The plumbers were still in her home, repairing the now falling apart bathroom in the condominium she had been renting for the past eight years. I told her not to worry and to take her time.

I waited with the pleasurable company of a slice of banana chocolate cake and a cup of skinny cappuccino. When she arrived, the storytelling began as she worked her way through a tall stack of banana pancakes with bacon. She is one of those people where eating a sweet dish must be complemented by a salty or savory dish to balance off the flavours. In this case, the salty bacon did the trick.

Her Story

People are often bigger risk takers at a younger age. This was the case for Rachel. More than 16 years ago, on 14 January 1993, she took the biggest leap into the unknown. She embarked on a new life in Singapore, not knowing any relatives or friends in this island. She had not been here before or any other Asian country. But she had been to Switzerland to visit her aunt and uncle living there. From there she traveled around to Belgium, Germany, Austria, and the UK for two months.

Rachel was then 22 years old. A recent graduate of journalism, she had a stable job working for an employment agency and writing freelance on the side. For six months, she worked for a PR firm, with its biggest client based in Singapore. The client was so pleased with her work that they created a job for her in Singapore. With nothing much to lose, she figured it made sense to try out a new life in this foreign land. She shares her philosophy with me, "My one goal in life is to reduce the number of regrets I have in my death bed." She explains, "I would have so much respect for myself even if I didn't like it, because I would have known for sure. At least I tried." She was not thinking of a long-term arrangement. In her mind, it was just a two-year stint.

Nothing prepared her for her first year in Singapore. Not knowing anyone, her boss rented her a room in Jurong with a Chinese family who didn't speak English. "I really felt like I was alone." Rachel describes the period as "the loneliest and most blessed, most grace-drenched time of my life."

The change coming from a very social environment in the Philippines, where you are always surrounded by a hive of activity and always in the company of friends, into her new life alone in Singapore was too drastic. "When you grow up in the Philippines, you never watch movies alone. You never go to the restroom alone. There's always someone to go with you. And then suddenly, there was just you. That was so glaring and startling for me," she states as a matter of fact.

This new experience of loneliness hit her deeply. "I was never alone. And suddenly, I was thrust into it. I had no recourse but to cling to God." She remembers, "When I look at that year, it was very painful. You know when people say you have to go through the fire. That was a bit of going through the fire." When she tells her colleagues then of that phase in her life, they find it hard to believe she was going through an emotionally difficult time. She performed perfectly at work. But they had no idea she was crying everyday. "The reason I was ok was that I could let it out in the morning and in the evening." She admits, "I'm a wallower. If I miss my family, that's where I am. So I just had to go through with it. There are problems you solve, and there are problems you go through. And that was something I just had to go through."

This sad phase is not something Rachel would wish on anybody. On hindsight she realizes, "When I moved here, I was young and brash. I didn't know that was coming for me. If you told me, I wouldn't probably have taken the job offer."

But despite her sadness and loneliness, young Rachel did not lose hope. She turned to God in prayer. "Everyday I would bug God. I would say, 'You know Lord I have no friends here.' I kept bugging him and bugging him, until I think he got fed up."

"One day I was crossing the street in Yishun and I saw this girl who looked like any other local. I said to myself, 'oh, she looks like my grade school and high school friend Persh…Persh? Oh gosh I think it is Persh.' I figured there was nothing to lose since I did not know anyone here. I shouted her name. 'PERSH!' She then looked at me and answered in true Pinoy fashion, 'Hoy!'" Not only did Rachel find a friend, they both agreed to become roommates and share a place with other Filipinos.

Sixteen years ago, Singapore was very different from the way it is now. Rebecca recalls, "Then you would only hear Tagalog spoken on the streets of the city on Sunday, when the domestic helpers had their day off." The number of Filipinos working in Singapore was not as large as it is today. Even getting around was more difficult then. There was no purple line then and the red line ended in Yishun, making many portions of northern Singapore not as easily accessible.

After two years working for the company that brought her to Singapore, she decided it was time for a change. It was December 1994 then, and she gave herself until the end of February to find a job. She continued her conversation with God, telling him, "Basically, if you want me to stay here, you'll give me a job. If you don't want me to stay, don't give me a job. Not that I wanted to give him an ultimatum, but sometimes it is really simple. I think we just complicate it." It was crystal clear in her head. Everyday she offered her prayers, and did her share in the deal. "I said, 'You will let me know. My job is to find what the options are here and apply to them. You will turn up and let me know.'"

She went to numerous lukewarm interviews. But when she went to this company called Asian Business News (now called CNBC) for a job as a PR coordinator, she knew with certainty it was the job for her. She boldly told the interviewer, "I'm telling you now, I want this job. I can do it. I can make it work. I will own it. But it's up to you if you want to give it to me." She walked away surprised at what she had just done. Yet there was clarity within her, "I knew it was where I was supposed to be. It is a rare thing for me to be sure. I am almost always unsure. So when I'm sure it's odd. It's a red letter day for me when I have no doubt."

With her 28 February deadline coming up, there was still no job offer. She was getting anxious and worried. "Because God has a wicked sense of humor, he held on till the last. I was always Ms. Positivity, knowing that God always take care of me and that he continues to take care of me." This one time she said to God, "Can I just not be Positivity Girl today? Tomorrow I'll get back. But today I really just want to feel bad." To her surprise, the HR Manager called that day and offered her the job.

On 7 March 1995, she started with CNBC, staying there for seven years. The pay TV industry was then very young, so she knew most of the people in this tightly knit circle. She was offered a job in ESPN, where she stayed for two years. Disney Channel offered her a job, where she has been working for five years now.

Rachel has gone through the whole gamut of emotions and experiences in Singapore. Upon arriving, it reminded her of Switzerland for its efficiency. Just like the precision of the Swiss, in this Switzerland of Asia, you could expect the buses to arrive on time. She noticed at work how her colleagues were task oriented compared to the more laid-back ways of Filipinos. "*Merienda* (snacking) is central to the Filipino work life, so it's impossible to have a meeting without food in the Philippines." In contrast, Singaporeans in her eyes seemed very bookish. "Most of them don't know how easy they have it here. And many are not street smart." Yet she thoroughly enjoys working with Singaporeans, making good friends with many of her colleagues.

In the beginning, she lived with a Chinese family who could not communicate with her in a HDB unit in Jurong. She had to decipher the unique ways of living in a HDB flat, such as the special art of hanging the heavy poles to dry her clothes outside the building. When living with her friends in Yishun, a walkman, cash and some jewelry where stolen from their HDB unit, allegedly by some migrant worker who entered through the window while they were at work. For the past eight years, she happily resides in the East Coast area, sharing a home with her hotelier sister.

Being a Filipino woman in Singapore, she is often mistaken as a maid. Cab drivers would make comments like "Ah, your boss is good, ah, Saturday is day off." She would just say, "ya, employer very nice." She realizes it is an honest mistake on their part. On one occasion, she took the MRT along with a Chinese-Filipino friend and another Filipina friend. An old Chinese couple told her Chinese Filipino friend that she was such a nice employer for bringing her maids out.

Sometimes, she is mistaken for a Malay. At the hawker stalls, they sometimes refuse to serve her pork dishes. She tries to explain that she is not Muslim, but this kind soul says, "I try to explain, but these uncles love Allah so much. So I just move and order fish ball noodles or something else next door. I don't fight it anymore."

The most common question she gets from fellow Filipinos is "*Saan ka nag-tatrabaho?*" (Where do you work?). Singaporeans ask her a different question, "What do you do on weekends?" This was more prevalently asked many years ago when she was new in Singapore. "Like I'm alien and very different from them. They assume I do interesting things. They ask less now, since there are more foreigners in Singapore. It's as if they are so bored here, they can't imagine what we foreigners do with our free time."

Rachel has made many friends in Singapore. Weekends are no longer lonely for her. She has choir on Saturdays, and for the past seven years, she has been practicing yoga. She religiously attends her yoga class on Sundays. This homebody has also taken an interest in baking. With the spirit of a young child, she happily enjoys her job at Disney Channel, catering to kids' viewing pleasures. She also finds much purpose in her life, as she is deeply committed to funding the mortgage of the family home in the Philippines (which they had lost in a court case several years ago). This Christ-centered Catholic has yet to find love in Singapore. She tells me, "There is nothing more attractive than a man who loves God." She wittingly adds, "As long as he's not a priest!"

Rachel describes her initial coming to Singapore as her season in the desert. She elaborates, "It was like getting my PhD in faith, skipping all the years needed to obtain a Masters." What she has now is a very special, intimate relationship with God. "He is more patient than anything. If you ask me to describe my relationship with God in one word—it is gingerly. That's how he leads me." She explains that God is very gentle in coaxing her. And for the forty days of Lent, she successfully gave up caffeine. "I know in my mind I can take it up. I have the freedom. I can take up coffee anytime, and he won't love me any less."

While she still experiences moments of solitude, Rachel does not feel the intense loneliness as she had when she first arrived. "I only feel lonely after I go home to the Philippines for Christmas. I come back to Singapore, and all of a sudden I don't hear my family's voices or the dogs barking." Each year in January, she reflects on how she feels about living in Singapore. Despite having a Permanent Resident status, she asks herself annually if she still wishes to stay.

I ask her whether this is the home where she belongs. She ponders, "That's a tough question." With her family in the Philippines and her best friend in New York, the people who anchor her are not in Singapore. She has found herself thinking once when the plane landed in Changi Airport, "I'm home."

Whether she belongs to this home, she gives a complex explanation: "I'm used to being left of field. I'm always in the fringe, never in the center of the circle. That's how my life is here. I'm never going to be one of them. And when I'm home in the Philippines, I'm not one of them either. I don't know all these celebrities anymore. I don't know these songs back home, after 16 years of being away. I'm always an odd fit. I'm not local. Put me in any crowd and I will hold my own. It is a weird place to be in. I think there are very few people who live in our zip code. I'm single with no kids. I'm always the odd one out. But it's not uncomfortable anymore. I think it's a choice you make. You can always make it uncomfortable for youself. It's just an odd place, but it is not a bad place."

She then relates it back to her closest friend. "Even Jesus had no place to lay his head, so who else better to understand." What will happen next remains a mystery. She joyfully surrenders what the future holds to Her Dearest Friend, "I will give God wiggle room to surprise me."

11 *Two Degrees of Separation*

John Lee, American
Accenture Partner, Married with children,
Moved to Singapore in September 2007

How We Met

It is natural to look for the familiar in a foreign land. I immediately adjusted to getting around on the MRT. Living seven stops away from Orchard on the red line, I instantly memorized the stops along the way. Two stops along the MRT that made me feel right at home: Orchard and City Hall. There is a happy energy in Orchard, where tourists and shops happily mingle. And I'm one of those geeks who gets a high from the scent of new books. On any bad day, bring me to Borders and I will be in a blissful state, pouring through books and magazine for hours.

City Hall linking the green and red line became a frequent stop for me. Whenever I had to go to my editors' offices in Amoy Street, I had to pass through City Hall to get to Tanjong Pagar. The Starbucks just above the MRT station was a convenient place to sit and get my thoughts together. The only problem is that the coffee house is often jam packed with non-coffee drinkers just sitting on the chairs. Also, sharing a table doesn't seem to be the norm here.

One afternoon, I had just finished a meeting with my British editor. My mind was still racing with ideas from our meeting. With no seat available, I spotted an executive sitting solo at one of the tables. I asked if I could share a table and he was agreeable. I then proceeded to make sense of my notes from my meeting with my editor, jotting down my thoughts. The guy I was sharing a table with seemed very intense, with his eyebrows furrowed. I moved away a bit, fearing this seemingly unfriendly guy. As he talked on the phone, the intensity of the stress in his life was tangible. And then he asked if he could borrow a pen. I lent him my pen, and when he returned it, he asked me if I knew where a certain spa was. He said he was scheduled to get a massage. I told him I was new in the city and didn't know where that was. He then asked where I was from. "The Philippines," I said. Smiling, he told me his wife was Filipina as well. He was an American from Chicago, but he was about to move to Singapore.

We chatted a bit more, and eventually exchanged cards. His name is John Lee, a partner in his 50s from Accenture.

I forgot about my encounter with John. I went on with my life, worked full-time for a magazine, left that job, started my own company, had a Belgian boyfriend, and broke up with the boyfriend. But I found another Starbucks, also in Raffles City, a newly opened outlet with less people and a bright happy aura. It was tucked along Raffles Tower, just across Chijmes. I was again lost in thought, this time writing an article for a magazine. And to my surprise, walking my way was a guy on the phone. His eyes opened wide, and he said, "Maida?" It was John Lee, and he was now living in Singapore.

His office was located on the 33rd floor of the same building as the coffee house.

This Starbucks became my home away from home in Singapore. When I was going bonkers writing from home, I came here for my caffeine fix and also for its feel-good ambiance. The baristas here were refreshingly friendly. They truly made their customers feel welcomed. On my lowest day in Singapore, I barely had any sleep after my boyfriend had broken up with me. All my friends were at work. To make it worse, I had to meet a deadline for an editor. But as the emotions swelled up inside me, I took a break from my writing. I asked the barista to watch my things as I needed to get some fresh air and go for a walk. I headed to the Cathedral two blocks away and cried my eyes out. After a while, I gained my composure and returned to the café. I ordered another cup of coffee. When the barista asked how I was doing, tears came rolling down my eyes. The store manager, a big friendly guy called Wan, then sat down next to me. He gave me a Starbucks key chain and started talking about the beaches in the Philippines, and soon the tears stopped. I was smiling again. And from that moment that Starbucks became my office. When words no longer flowed from my head onto paper, I would head here and write. It was a comfortable place where I could channel my second wind.

On several occasions, John and I would see each other here. This particular store had its own community, regulars who dropped by everyday: Sam a graphic designer, Eleanor a health writer who specialized in aging, several students, and a pilot.

John would always ask how I was doing. He was witty and comfortably engaged in spontaneous conversations, as most Americans are. Knowing I was single, he would often ask how my love life was going. He would then offer unsolicited advice on men, telling me to have several men to meet my different needs. And in true Singapore fashion, as we talked about boxing and fitness one day, I learned that John and my friend Joy, a Filipina architect, were boxing in the same gym. It turned out John was one of the owners of the gym. In fact, he and Joy had sparred once. Joy even punched his nose. Again it proves that in Singapore, it is not six degrees of separation but only two.

On another occasion, John was particularly excited to see me. As I paid for my cappuccino and he waited for his macchiato, he exclaimed, "I have a story for you! There's this big news in our condo, two guys left their wives for their maids…." His wife was shocked. And I probed deeper, "Are the maids Filipinas? What about the wives?" His wife was upset. He teased his wife saying, "What's wrong with that, you don't want other fellow Filipinas to get out of the ricefields?"

That was John and his naughty humor. And then he had to leave to run off for another appointment. My interaction with him was limited to quick exchanges in Starbucks. Once he had a big grin on his face. He saw my extremely colorful Indian skirt, then he said, "Are you going back to your tribal roots? I saw a skirt like that in *National Geographic*." "But this is Indian and I'm Filipino," I retorted. He then went on to tell me that he had seen a *National Geographic* feature on tribal people and printed a photo of the tribe and made some joke about them being his wife's ancestors, and posted them around the house just to annoy her.

His Story

With many business trips abroad, pining John down for an interview was a challenge. But on my third try, I finally nailed him down.

We finally meet at the American Club, a members-only country club on Claymore Hill which John is a new member of. Dressed casually in a T-shirt, shorts, and leather moccasins, Singapore's tropical climate seems to be suited for this top executive. He waits for my taxi to arrive, and ushers me into this exclusive club. He asks if I had been in here before, to which I shake my head. He tells me it is less posh than the Tanglin Club.

I soak it all in. A few people are swimming laps mid-day, and there are a number of businessmen seated with a view of the pool, tapping away on their laptops. John gets us each a cup of coffee. This no-nonsense executive has his blackberry and his mobile phone on standby, with his earpiece and microphone all set, as he awaits for important phone calls from all around the world. It feels as though we are in a relaxing resort off on some island, but in reality, Orchard Road is only a few steps away.

John moved to Singapore on September 2007, with his wife and sons aged seven and ten following a few months after. Born in the mid-west and educated in Michigan State, his adult life has been on the go as an expatriate. He lived in Los Angeles for 15 years, six years in London, four years in Chicago, before moving to Singapore.

This is his first posting in Asia. And Asia, being the next frontier, provides many business opportunities as a partner in one of the top consulting companies in the world. It also helped that his other half was very open to relocating the family to Singapore.

The first thing John wishes to correct is how Singapore is often called "Asia for Beginners". He finds it pseudo-derogatory. "I think it doesn't give credit to what I realized. Singapore has a really strong, unique culture." He is quick to disagree with the notion of many that the country is highly Westernized. He gives the heads up, "Before you come and just think that it is London Lite or New York Lite, it is not. It is a unique culture."

He has obviously thought about it and processed it in his head. Basing it on his varied experiences conducting business in Europe, US, Asia, and Australia, John observes a close-knit pervasive culture in existence. He explains: "The culture is so strong. Highly networked. Highly educated. Everybody knows everybody it seems. The Six Degrees of Separation phrase does not apply here. It's really about two."

He expands on this, "I have this small theory that one reason why New York and London are so successful is that there's a lot of people all together in one place. And ideas are going like this (makes a gesture with his hands going around). So ideas get tossed around. It is a highly networked, highly evolved type of information flow in a society. In Singapore, it is more condensed. It's a small community. It's two degrees of separation. But you've got pretty sharp people here. The expatriates and the locals are highly functioning individuals. And in close proximity, you can get to meet them very quickly."

Returning from his last business trip from the US, he notices the ease of life in his compact new homeland. "I was back in Chicago last week and I was struck by how much easier it is in Singapore in some ways. You can get more things done here. In Chicago, I had to drive everywhere to do anything. Here, you can walk to do many things."

Drawing from first-hand experience, John makes a very interesting point. "In bigger cities like London or Paris, it is harder to meet people than it is here….much harder. The expatriate community is more spread out in those places. Here it is more condensed. And people are more willing to meet people here. So I find that it is easier to move to Singapore than those expatriate places."

In fact his move here was even easier than moving to another city in the US. He tells me, "To be honest we moved from London to Chicago—the wife is from Chicago—but we did not meet any new people. It was very hard. I didn't find it easy to make connections in the States. People are very busy there."

Moving to Singapore was a breeze for John, describing it as "water off a duck's back". His two sons also settled in quickly. In fact, he rarely sees his 10-year-old-son on weekends, but he is not complaining. "My son sleeps over at one friend's house on a Friday night, then sleeps over at another friend's house on Saturday night. He shows up in our house with someone else's clean clothes." But he doesn't worry about his son's safety. The independent boy can take a taxi from his school in Woodlands to their home near Nassim Road. His parents also feel comfortable to let him walk alone on Orchard Road, except on Sundays when it is too busy.

Recognizing the importance of a social network in helping his children to settle in a new place, John gives this advice to other expatriate parents, "Where you put your kids to school is most important. Because they have to be in a school enviroment where they get a good network." He is very happy with the Singapore American School. It has known to be the top international school in the country, but John notes from other friends and colleagues that the Australian International School is very good as well. He even shares a growing trend for some expatriates to send their children to some of the higher end local schools.

Not only does the school provide a good education for his sons, they too have the privilege of a more ethnic diverse school population than they normally would have in a school in the US. The social network does not end with his kids, parents also become highly networked as well through the international school. The same close-knit culture follows, "There's a joke we have at the Singapore American school that whatever it is don't volunteer for anything, because if you volunteer for one thing, you've just volunteered for five things. If you volunteer to hold the flags on the sidelines, you're bound to be the coach as well. They grab everyone in. It's a very tightly networked environment."

While weekdays are packed with high-powered meetings and conference calls, you will find John participating in his sons' sports on Saturdays, including basketball, soccer, and baseball. He volunteered to be the team manager for his son's baseball team, only to find out later that he too would be the referee in the game.

His wife has also settled nicely in Singapore, even volunteering for a women's center. The contribution of expatriate women to local society is often overlooked. But as I volunteer in groups like the SPCA and RDA, I am impressed with the many expatriate wives who are deeply involved in helping the disabled, or providing more humane conditions for dogs and cats.

Keenly observing his adopted home, John calls Singaporeans "uber-urban people". Despite it being a small city, they act as if they live in one of the mega cities in Asia. John is fascinated by his observations, "They don't go for a drive. In the States, you have this ethic that you go to the countryside, and in the Philippines too." He expands. "They're an urban people. The countryside is Orchard Road. It's not like the French, who go to the South of France." Add to that the interesting facet that a majority of the population lives in government-subsidized housing, the HDBs.

But John is not all complaining about his life in Singapore. He loves the ease of getting around by walking or taking a cab. He has been a boxing aficionado since his stint in London. Here in Singapore, he is one of the investors in a boxing gym in MacPherson Road, where he trains three times a week. John and our common friend Joy have been trying to convince me to give it a go, and perhaps lose some pounds and get fit along the way. Many months later, I still haven't given it a try. "One of these days," I keep telling them.

Even in matters of food, he cannot complain. It is a fact though that Western food is more expensive. But John makes a clear point that cheap delicious food is easily accessible in Singapore, "I was out very late last night and I had a stunning meal for $3.50. Dining next to me was a Russian hooker and a woman flaunting her diamonds too!"

Perhaps the best asset of this compact city can also be a liability to many expatriates. John warns about getting set into the routine. "You walk into Orchard. You go to your club. You don't see the local life, and you don't have to because Singapore is so organized." John points out its efficiency, "You can land at Changi Airport and get to your house in the record time of an hour."

This top management consultant excels in making many businesses work. Being a partner in Accenture and a seasoned expatriate living in different locations with ease, I ask for advice he can give foreigners choosing to move to Singapore. Again John emphasizes, "Singapore has a culture that's derived from the small sized, highly networked and highly educated people, a busy trading enviroment, and is very Asian. It is important to find your niche here." For John, his work, his children's school, and his small boxing gym business have provided him with valuable networks. He wisely advises expatriates, "You need to find a niche to make friends, you need to find your hook, be it golf, flower-arranging etc. You need to find whatever it takes."

While lost in thoughts in the company of my cup of coffee and the words I am weaving into magazine articles, I welcome the quick encounters I have with John at Starbucks. Many Singaporeans will not easily engage in conversation with strangers as Westerners do. As a people person, I miss that human connection. I miss the randomness of it all.

John spots me once again as I am writing this book. He asks how it's going, then tells me how he loves being a global citizen and how wonderful it is to move to a new place. If anything, he regrets not learning how to speak Chinese.

I agree immensely with John's wise advise in finding a niche. As the chapters unfold, you will discover that my life in Singapore has been made richer by people who share the same interests as I have: be it singing in a choir, working for a magazine, enjoying the sunset, or in the case of my relationship with John, in drinking copious amounts of coffee at Starbucks.

12 *Finding His Balance*

Shawn Kiyotaka Lee Fukuzaki, Japanese
36 years old, Art Director,
Moved to Singapore in 2006, Single

How We Met

People who know me well are aware I am hopeless when it comes to my sense of direction. Having made plans to have dinner with my friend Shawn at Bon Gout, a Japanese restaurant in Robertson Quay, I was stumped which direction it was. I had been to Robertson Quay before, but could not remember clearly how to get there. I walked from Raffles City Shopping Center at City Hall, asking some Singaporeans working in the mall for directions. One had no clue where Robertson Quay was. Another told me it was next to Gallery Hotel and it would take a 30-minute walk. I knew there was a bus heading that way. He pointed to the taxi stand just outside the store, and suggested I take a cab instead. No way would I take a taxi in the city during the peak hour unless I really had to. So I proceeded to take my long walk.

My head was filled with thoughts. I wondered why many Singaporeans do not know their country well. It is such a compact island, yet many times when I ask for directions, people don't seem to know where things are. It gets really disturbing when the street I'm looking for happens to be just one street away, yet they don't even know that. On one occasion, I was looking for a building and the waiter had to ask his manager where it was, only to tell me that it was the very building the restaurant was in. I wondered if the government's efforts in creating new self-sufficient towns has resulted in residents moving only within a small area in close proximity to their homes. One Muslim lady was shocked that I knew my way around more than she did, even though I was not a local.

The walk took me down North Bridge Road, passing through Funan Mall, Boat Quay and Clarke Quay. It was a Monday night and the restaurants and bars were not too busy. But there were still tourists taking photos by the river, with the pastel-coloured buildings of Clarke Quay in the background. There were joggers having their early evening run, tuned into the songs playing on their iPods.

I started thinking about Shawn and how our beautiful friendship blossomed. Shawn and I worked for the same in-flight magazine, but we never really worked together for he was the Art Director to the Japanese version of the magazine, while I was the Travel & Lifestyle Editor of the English title. Shawn is a 36-year-old Japanese graphic designer. We both worked within the confines of the "fish tank", a glass enclosure separating us from the other employees of this magazine company. When I arrived and walked into the fish tank on my third day of work, Shawn smiled at me and asked me what he could do for me, thinking I was a visitor. He had just returned from his holidays. Later that day, this pleasant guy walked from table to table handing out Mamee noodle snacks and a few pieces of coconut candy he bough in Ipoh, Malaysia, where he spent his holidays. The thoughtfulness and cheerfulness felt awfully familiar, very much like a lot of Filipinos. I then learned he was Shawn. The previous day over lunch, the editorial staff of a home design title were gushing over him. They said he offered free yoga classes for the company employees every Thursday lunchtime.

I love yoga and Pilates, and definitely wanted to join his class. But with the hectic schedule of my job, I did not have the luxury of having a lunch break. My lunch routine often involved the graphic designers kindly purchasing food for me and my fellow editors to save us some time. I would then spend the lunch hour sitting in front of my computer, still working, editing and checking on copy.

One Thursday, I finally had the opportunity to try Shawn's yoga class. It was conducted in the building's function room. There we laid out our yoga mats and followed every word Shawn uttered. His gentle ways were soothing. But he was firm enough to motivate each individual to achieve the correct posture and pose. There were only four or five people in the class, all women. One or two aunties would tell Shawn they could not do one pose or another due to bad backs or a sprained hand. And in his most diplomatic way, Shawn knew how to push them to perform to their level.

After an hour of yoga and sweating it out, we quickly grabbed a quick lunch of fish noodle soup from the Chinese concessionaire in our canteen before heading back to our desks. On one occasion, I was the only student who showed up for the yoga class, turning it into a special one-on-one lesson. With Shawn's 100 percent focus on me, he corrected my posture and poses. I didn't realize I had been cheating on many of the moves and Shawn showed me how to do it correctly. And we would repeat it until I finally did it right. It was the most difficult yoga class I had, with my body aching in places I didn't know existed before, and I sweated profusely. On this occasion, we ate in the nicest restaurant on our street, which was a steak house with tacky decor serving Western food. And there we freely talked about our lives. We became each other's confidantes in the office. Shawn lived in Bishan, two stops away from my Yio Chu Kang home and only a few bus stops away from my place. Shawn became literally the closest friend to me. All my other friends lived in the East Coast region or close to the city.

Shawn lived close to MacRitchie Reservoir, and he spent every weekend going for a jog or walk though the dense natural environment. He invited me to join him for a walk one early Sunday morning. We first loaded on energy for the long nature walk with some bagels and coffee in one of the cafes in Bishan Junction. We each bought a large bottle of water to keep us hydrated and we were off. As MacRitchie Reservoir unveiled its natural beauty and attractions to us, Shawn and I freely opened up about intimate details of our lives, covering everything from work to love, religion, family, and the intricacies of life. We did the Tree Top Walk, a 250-meter aerial walkway on a high suspension bridge over the forest. Being 25 meters off the ground, we got a great view of the forest canopy, watching birds, monkeys and the panoramic view of Upper Peirce Reservoir. We continued walking through the trail around the entire reservoir. There were a number of monkeys freely roaming, unafraid of the people jogging or walking. I enjoyed watching them from a distance as they climbed trees and swung on dangling vines. But when the monkeys came close to me, I would freeze. The gentle ways of Shawn would ease me from my fears, and he would kindly walk very close to me, protecting me from any potential harm from the monkeys.

After four hours of walking through the different paths in MacRitchie and talking the entire way, Shawn and I were definitely bonded. My legs were so tired and ready to collapse, yet we managed to hop on a bus and have a big hearty lunch. Shawn recommended the Kampung Chicken at Upper Thomson Road. The chicken pieces were moist, paired with stir-fried bean spouts and rice, and it was the most comforting and satisfying lunch shared with my newfound friend.

More and more Shawn and I became real friends to each other at work, and outside of work. My first trip to Arab Street was to celebrate his 35th birthday with a select group of friends at a restaurant in Haji Lane. The colorful shophouses and bohemian energy reminded me of the hip Malate district in Manila, known for its quaint restaurants, colourful clientele of artsy and gay patrons, and a vibrant night scene.

Together, Shawn and I attended special discounted talks and tour of the Nalanda Buddhist trail exhibit at the Asian Civilization Museum. And when my parents came to visit from Manila, Shawn joined my two other friends to partake of an authentic home-cooked Filipino meal. He thoroughly enjoyed sampling unfamiliar cuisines and shed a genuine interest in the religion and culture of the Filipinos.

Living close by to each other, we could easily meet for dinner at Upper Thomson. Shawn shared his discovery of Part 1 Café, a quaint café serving stews, beer, and a generous collection of travel books and magazine available for reading. It was an unpolished yet soothing place where you could kick back aad relax for hours. Together, we sampled the food at an Indian-Italian Restaurant, then we had tea while everyone else around us had beer in an unexpectedly hip watering hole in Upper Thomson called Liquid Kitchen.

As I walked along the river in search of Clarke Quay, the wonderful memories continued to surface. Thinking it was too far, I again asked a guy for directions. He didn't know. Then finally Gallery Hotel was visible. I sent Shawn a text messages that I was near, asking for directions to the restaurant. He said, "It's near the colorful bridge." What many people describe as the colourful bridge or to some the aboriginal bridge is actually made by the Filipino artist Pacita Abad. Shawn was standing on the opposite of the bridge, waiting for me. And as I smiled with pride as I walked through the bridge, I reveled in the bright reds, yellows, blues, and greens, and the cheerful patterns my fellow Filipino created, adding her unique stamp to Singapore's urban landscape.

His Story

People have varied reasons for moving to a foreign country. But for Shawn, living abroad has become a way of life. Coming from a mixed marriage with a Japanese dad and a Malaysian-Chinese mother, from the Kinta Valley, close to Ipoh, his life had been a blend of cultures. Shawn, born in Tokyo, spent most of his childhood in Yokohama, 30 minutes away from Tokyo and Chiba, close to Narita. This artist lived in the United States for three years while studying graphic design at the Fashion Institute of Technology and spent some time in the Orange County, yes the OC. He enjoyed residing in the OC in the company of its very conservative, dominantly white community. What he loved the most being there were the stunning views of the Pacific Ocean. After his stint in the US, this free spirit moved back to Tokyo. But after six months, he just knew with certainty that he no longer belonged in his hometown.

When he was offered a job as a graphic artist for a magazine in Shanghai, he grabbed the opportunity. He settled nicely into this cosmopolitan city, finding his own niche with the bohemian artsy community, as well as love in his South African partner. Together, they lived right smack in the heart of the city at the French Concession. He also worked as a yoga teacher in one of the clubs in the city. His good looks, gentle ways, and fluency in Mandarin easily endeared him to the hip and young clientele of the club.

His South African partner did not speak Mandarin and did not enjoy living in Shanghai. He preferred to move to Singapore, and the love-struck Shawn did not mind moving for his loved one. He also had relatives in Singapore, visiting often with his mother for holidays.

But despite his familiarity with Singapore, living in the Lion City was very different from merely coming here for a visit. The move from Shanghai to Singapore was not smooth. From their hip digs in the French concession at the heart of Shanghai, he and his partner settled in a HDB unit in Telok Blangah, not exactly hip nor at the center of the city.

Most difficult to get used to was the oppressive heat. All his life, Shawn had always lived in places with four seasons. He missed the change of seasons. The details in the seasons allowed Shawn to remember details of his life. His memories were so intertwined with the cherry blossom season in spring, or a very cold day in winter. For the first three months, he found the tropical heat very tiring. It was made worse by the extreme contrast when he entered the very cold buses and offices.

In a society that valued a single focus of specialization, it was difficult for this talented artist to find a job suited for his unique skills. He applied to several gyms in Singapore, but the focus of yoga was more of an exercise here rather than a spiritual experience. He even approached a headhunter to seek assistance in finding a job, but his diverse skills were frowned upon. During these months, he missed the support of his eclectic mix of friends. Add to that pressure the unraveling of his relationship with his South African partner.

After some time, Shawn was hired as the art director for *Silver Kris*, the in-flight magazine of Singapore Airlines. With his job in place, Shawn slowly picked up the pieces of his life. After three months, he learned to accept and live with the oppressive heat in Singapore. He loved all the food offerings in the city, although he found good Japanese food to be overpriced. He took on the Chinese practice of eating "heaty" and "cooling" food. He limited his intake of heaty food and indulged more in cooling food, suitable for the warm climate.

Despite living in Shanghai, NY, Tokyo and LA, Shawn found Singapore to be noisy and claustrophobic. It was due to the small size of the island, compressing the noise and activities in a smaller space. In his HDB in Telok Blangah, he was close to the highway, hearing the loud buzz of cars going by. He found joy in nature, taking long walks at MacRitchie. Living in a HDB flat immersed Shawn in the heartland, the real Singapore experience of seeing funeral wakes, Hungry Ghost Festival events, and weddings held at the void decks of the flats. But three months ago, he discovered a cozy home that suited his quiet and laid-back nature. Shawn now lives in a black and white colonial home in a former British officer's residence in Changi Village. He does not mind the long journey to get home from the city, requiring him to take the MRT all the way to Tanah Merah, and a 20-minute bus ride. On his birthday, it took me over an hour to get to his place, while another friend took two hours to get there.

But once in Changi, he can kick back his worries and happily relax. Taking a jog by the oft-empty boardwalk of Chang Point is the perfect ending to his days. There are the small restaurants in Changi Village, where he and I shared a pitcher of Sangria in the afternoon and bites of tapas, the famous *nasi lemak* store in the hawker center, and the easily accessible Pulau Ubin. It's actually easier for Shawn to go to Ubin than it is to go to the city. It is the kampung lifestyle he loves about Changi and the greenery found in many parts of Singapore.

To address missing the bohemian feel of the bigger cities he lived in, Shawn has found neighborhoods that stimulate his artful soul. He loves the chill out vibe in the lanes and shops of Kampung Glam. And he loves little India for its very colorful, raw, and unpolished feel. But he'd be quick to point out that he doesn't like Chinatown. He says, "it feels fake."

When he feels utterly claustrophobic, Shawn heads off to nearby destinations. He has traveled to Chang Mai and Bangkok in Thailand and has explored the many crevices of Malaysia, including Pulau Tioman, frequent trips to KL to visit friends, and visiting Ipoh for great food and to see his aunt. Ipoh is a special place for Shawn as this is close to where his mother grew up. When the pressure at work was just immense, Shawn confided that he did an impromptu adventure alone to one of the Indonesian islands close by to simply get away from it all.

He has found a good mix of friends by indulging in his different interests. Shawn began learning how to speak Thai, and now he is learning to play the keyboard. He was also involved in acting in a documentary on expats.

Listening to Shawn's story, it becomes clear that life is about making choices. While choosing where you live is crucial, finding your balance and creating the life you want is more important. It becomes a choice of what you indulge in and what you do. As much as he enjoys shopping, you will not likely find Shawn in any of the Singapore malls on weekends. "Singapore offers less choices than in Tokyo, where I can go from town to town just to buy sneakers." But now he chooses to buy less and finds himself shopping only when he travels. Working for a demanding publication, he tells me that he is no longer as easy-going as he used to.

Most fascinating for Shawn is that he is finding his roots in Singapore. From the first time we met, he had huge hesitations about getting his PR, not certain he would like to live here for long. But after two years of working here, he now is in the process of applying for his PR. Singapore is where his Japanese father met his Malaysian Chinese mother. He was learning to speak Mandarin and in the process he found his true love. It is also the same country Shawn is now finding his balance.

As I gaze at Shawn sitting alfresco in a Japanese bookstore cum restaurant, behind him Pacita Abad's bridge illuminates brightly at night. The bridge made by a non-Singaporean has become an icon in Singapore. I look at Shawn, a vibrant, warm and cheerful artist who is finding his balance and his home in this country, and realize this is the changing face of Singapore.

13

Easy, Breezy Aussie

Sarah Porter, Australian,
36 years old, Sub-Editor,
Moved to Singapore in November 2008, Divorced

How We Met

Magazines are abundant in Singapore. There are over 70 English magazines produced in this city of over four million people. Hong Kong was once the hub of magazines produced in Asia, but Singapore seems to be the new publishing capital of the East.

While there are numerous titles published by Singapore companies, there are also the international titles. One such company is Ink Publishing, producing magazines like *Time Out Singapore* and a growing stable of inflight titles for airlines like Jetstar, Tiger Airways, Bangkok Airways, Cebu Pacific, and more. I had been writing for Ink for over a year prior to my move to Singapore.

Visiting their office during my travel to Singapore in March 2007, I was pleasantly enthralled by the company. Located on Amoy Street in Chinatown, the office is set in one of the cheerful colored shophouses. Inside, the cozy wooden floor sets the mood for a warm and friendly office. The editors are a merry mix of Brits, Aussies, a Canadian, some Singaporeans, and a Filipino. The mood is light and casual, with bantering and laughter.

But just like any other publishing company, there are deadly days when the next issue has to be closed. As one editor puts it, "It's just like finals week in school, when you have to put your life on hold. And time seems to stand still. Once it is over, your house is a huge mess, and you have to catch up on your life and your laundry."

With Ink offices in London and New York, the company here in Singapore is run with a global outlook. One of the editors I had worked closely with is Sarah Porter, putting together an extensive guide on Singapore for the Urban Redevelopment Authority (URA).

Her Story

Sarah Porter is a 36-year-old Australian, born in Toronto, Canada. Her father worked in the Air Force, and she lived in Darwin, Canberra, and Sydney as she was growing up. But it was in Sydney where Sarah spent 12 years, prior to moving to Jakarta for one year in 2007.

After finishing her Masters in Journalism, Sarah worked for the newspaper *The Jakarta Post* and *Weekender* magazine. After that, she moved to Singapore to be with her boyfriend. With a well-established network of Australian friends, moving here was easy. She instantly had a community. It also helped to have an instant place to call home in her boyfriend's place in Bukit Timah.

Bukit Timah is a favorite of foreigners. But it is not easily accessible by MRT. Sarah has to contend with taking a cab to the nearest MRT to get to work. She tells me it is a joy if you have a car. However, she frequently has to take a cab to get anywhere. But with her cheery outlook in life, most of the time she still enjoys long chats with cab drivers. Adding "lah" and calling them "uncle" makes the cabbies laugh and they all compliment her on her good Singlish. Their favorite topic is the ghost stories in the burial sites in Bukit Timah along Old Holland Road. All these horror stories has left the land empty, with no development wanting to build anything in this part of town. Not spooked by it, Sarah continues to jog here everyday. Beginning or ending her day with a jog in this part of town is a welcome getaway from the sometimes claustrophobic feeling she gets in Singapore.

Accustomed to wide-open spaces, this Aussie sometimes feels too cooped up in the city. She also misses the vibrant art scene in Sydney. Having a sister who is an actress, Sarah often watched plays and went to museums back in Australia. In Singapore, she has watched a few international shows at the Esplanade, but it does not quite have the same artsy vibe as her hometown.

Meeting up with Sarah one Thursday afternoon for a late lunch, I enter an unusually silent INK office. The tension in the room is palpable, with the editors' attention 100 percent focused on their screens. You could hear a pin drop and feel the tension in the air. It is the closing season for the magazine, Sarah explains as we walk out of the office into the warm sunny day. We settle on a Vietnamese restaurant just across Amoy Street Food Center.

"The great thing about working on Amoy Street is that there are so many good food options." Sarah exclaims, Aside from the two big hawker centers, there are excellent Thai, Vietnamese, Chinese, Indian and Italian restaurants in the area. While the steaming bowls of Pho are tempting, it just doesn't suit the sweltering heat. We settle on spring rolls with rice noodles for her, while I choose cold rice rolls. A regular in this small eatery, the uncle beams a big smile as he recognizes this tall, friendly Aussie girl.

When her bowl of noodles arrives, she pours a generous dallop of red chilli into it. She tucks in and her stressed mood quickly disappears. "Food makes me happy," she smiles like a little girl as the sun lights up the freckles on her face and her bouncy, curly hair.

After her year-long stint in Jakarta, settling in Singapore is a breeze. She loves the heat. But what she can't stand is the "kiasu" mentality of Singaporeans. She explains to me, "They always need to do better." She has seen this at work when she drives around Singapore, "Taxi drivers would always change lanes, just to be ahead of you." Even when waiting in the queue for a cab, she tells me how a woman annoyingly cut in front of her just to beat her in getting a cab." In Australia, it would be called keeping up with the Joneses. She tells me that many Singaporeans are embarrassed by how some of their own citizens act. When the airplane lands in Changi, many are pushing and shoving to be the first out of the airplane. This laid-back Aussie just sits there reading her book until everyone is out. She tells me, "It doesn't really matter. You have to wait for your luggage anyway, so why rush?"

Sarah and her gang of friends always manage to come up with activities to do and remain up to date and connected with events in their beloved Australia. With the recent bush fires in Australia, they had a fun evening of eating and drinking in Little India. Putting a tin for donations in the middle of the table, they had arm wrestling and other silly games. They even penalized you with a fine each time your phone rang. By the end of the evening, they raised $3,500.

Getting more fit and extending her social network, Sarah has joined a group of expat women who row in the Kallang River every Saturday. "It's probably the most difficult thing I've done. After practice, I have no energy to do anything else." On other weekends, Sarah gets away to Phuket and Langkawi, with plans to head to Vietnam, Laos, and Cambodia soon.

"There's more to Singapore than just expensive wine and chili crabs," says this informed editor. She lists Henderson Wave, Pulau Ubin and Pasir Ris as places worth checking out. Aussies love their wines, and Sarah is no different. She definitely misses the cheaper cost of alcohol, with a bottle going for $6 in Sydney. But trust this resourceful Aussie to find good deals on booze. "There's Wine Connection, where you can get a bottle of Rose for $24. Get a cheese platter, and you can have fun with your friends all night." She has also discovered the benefits of getting a membership card, which allows her to buy $5 San Miguel Beer at any Harry's, a popular pub found in many parts of Singapore.

When her sister came to visit, she showed her the traditional shophouses on Duxton Hill, the stunning view of the city from Swissotel's New Asia bar, and the mandatory stop at Long Bar at Raffles Hotel for a Singapore Sling (where it was invented). But it was condominium living that gave her Sydney-sider sister the biggest kick. "She wanted to experience it, so we hang out by the pool. She was amazed that it was like a hotel, with a lift, a pool, and all the amenities."

While shopping is huge in Singapore, for this laid-back Aussie, it is not a huge attraction. Her biggest purchase so far is a wet suit, gearing up for more diving adventures on her trips around Southeast Asia.

She reaches deep into her bowl of rice noodles, all the spices having collected at the bottom. Loving all things spicy, she is exhilarated. All revved up, her lunch hour is soon over and it is time to part.

We walk back to Amoy Street. As we give each other big hugs, she accidentally steps on the foot of a man walking by. "Sorry uncle," she says, only to realize it is a younger gentleman. "Oops, not an uncle," she laughs, then walks back to the frenzied life of a hardworking editor.

14

The Meek Lamb Turns to a Roaring Merlion

Stephen Harrowfield, New Zealand
34 years old, English as Second Language Teacher,
Moved to Singapore in July 2003, Single

How We Met

Achieving a good work-life balance is a tricky challenge, especially in Singapore, where being a workaholic seems to be an asset rather than a flaw. I had taken on a project to write a guide on Singapore, which required me to know details about where to eat, play, and explore in the north and east regions of the island. A lot of the attractions are man-made creations, like the national parks. Plunging deep into the project, I found myself weary from working. To meet the deadline, I was working even on weekends. For weeks, I was in the company of mostly my laptop and undertook solo excursions to explore the attractions. I needed local icons to interview, but surprisingly many were hesitant and fearful to be interviewed or photographed. Unlike in the Philippines or many Asian countries where total strangers I meet on the road would gladly help and pose for the cameras, here it was like a tooth extraction to get people to talk to me.

In the midst of madly trying to meet my deadline, my friend Isabel asked to borrow my digital voice recorder for an interview she had to do. I lent her my nifty tool and she returned it and treated me to dinner. As we sat at a *kopitiam* along Bencoolen, she told me about Singaporeexpats.com, a website where she met many interesting expats. As I dunked my garlic *naan* into the thick gravy of the butter chicken, I listened to her online dating adventures. Sitting close by the window, I caught a glimpse of a tall, yummy-looking Caucasian expat quickly walking out of his office building to grab dinner at the *kopitiam* and hurrying back into the office building. I realized at that moment how alienated I felt. My social life often revolved around gay men. I was initially shocked to find myself to be the lone straight person in a dinner party with gay men, but at the same time I felt right at home. We shared the same love for food, art, and music. Roaring, infectious laughter always filled our time together. We were easily endeared to each other, but it was never complicated. Yet being surrounded by gay men was probably not the best way for a single woman to meet single men. I took it as the cue to go back to online dating and explored this website.

For Isabel and many other expats, online dating has become an acceptable way of meeting people in Singapore. It eased my hesitation and fears of online dating. Perhaps I was a tad bit wary of the negative connotation for I had extensively studied mail-order brides for my dissertation in graduate school a few years back, and this pretty much felt like that.

With too much work occupying my mind for the past few weeks, I plunged into the adventure and logged onto the site. It is very much like shopping online, with the profiles spelling out many things you cannot really ask on a first date like weight, height, religion, and age. It allows you to narrow down a search based on degree or even eye color. I went through a few profiles.

One profile stood out. It read "I'm afraid I'm not a high-flying expat working for a large MNC (wish I were) but just an English teacher, so I'm afraid I can't wine and dine you every night…" The candidness and the humility was a breath of fresh air. We exchanged a few emails. His name is Steve, a 34-year-old single guy from New Zealand who works in Singapore as an ESL (English as a second language) teacher.

Just judging from our email exchange, I knew there was no romantic match for he is a meek and mild lamb while I am a fierce and feisty Leo. But one of his emails piqued my curiosity. He lamented how hard it was teaching ESL to mostly overseas Chinese students.

I asked if he was open to be interviewed for my book and he gladly agreed to a Saturday afternoon meeting after his morning tuition. I chose a quiet café in the Red Dot museum.

His Story

It is an ordinary hot Singapore afternoon. But when I walk out of Tanjong Pagar MRT, the rain is pouring. I had often been caught unprepared many times in the past by the sudden showers, causing me to walk home drenched to the amusement of the condominium guards. I soon learned that an umbrella is a staple in the bag of any commuter in Singapore.

I send Steve a text message when I arrive in the café. He arrives neatly dressed in a black striped polo shirt and jeans. The nervous energy is palpable. I break the ice by offering to get some coffee. He seems baffled by this lady's offer, but agrees to a latte.

As the rain pours outside and a handful of students do their work in the café, the conversation ensues. Saturday mornings for Steve, an ESL teacher for almost seven years, are usually spent teaching a Japanese couple. Tuition augments his salary as an ESL teacher in a private business school in the Kallang area.

This native of Christchurch, New Zealand, came to Singapore in hope of finding a job in the banking or finance sector. But with no luck in this sector, he saw an ad for a job teaching English in Korea. After a year of teaching in Korea, he returned to teach ESL in Singapore. His first four years were spent teaching ESL in a small business school near Bugis.

Unlike the stereotypical *ang mo* existence in Singapore, Steve lives more like a local. He first lived in the heartlands of Bishan. His home was a HDB unit next to Bishan Park, living amidst Singaporeans and close to many hawker centers. But a year later, Steve moved to a condominium in Simei. Moving in was like living in a resort. He recalls telling his mother back in Christchurch, "It's like I'm on holiday everyday of the year." His hometown has a milder climate with four seasons, and even the occasional snowy winters. Now in Singapore, he enjoys consistently warm, sunny days all year round.

Interestingly Christchurch is the same physical size as Singapore, but its population is only 350,000 compared to the over 4 million residents of the Lion City. On his first visit to Singapore, Steve was shocked that shopping malls were opened till 10 pm every day. In New Zealand, there is only one night when stores remain open till late, either a Friday night or a Saturday night. The rest of the week all the stores are closed by 5 pm.

But Steve easily adjusted to life in Singapore. He took the MRT and buses to get around. He also adapted to the hard-working lifestyle instilled here. His company did not allow for sick leave. One weekend he discovered a bit of a problem, "I completely lost my voice for three months and the doctor couldn't find out why. I woke up one day and walked down the street to a Burger King. When I wanted to order my food and opened my mouth to speak, nothing came out." Despite being unable to speak, his school still required him to teach.

Embracing the lifestyle of a workaholic, vacations were also practically non-existent for Steve. It was only a month ago that this Kiwi teacher had his first vacation in 10 years. He went to Phuket for the first time, enjoying the sun, sea, and seafood. It was an awakening. It made him vow to take more holidays to explore what Southeast Asia has to offer.

Steve also breaks the stereotype that all expats live and hang out in Holland Village. It was only last month that Steve first stepped foot in the spunky restaurant row loved by expats. Many expats love to cycle to Pulau Ubin, an island only 10 minutes away from Singapore. It is a quick getaway that seems to transport you back to the Singapore of many decades past. With a population of about a hundred people, the island has a village lifestyle, with small houses, backyards, and a community with neighbors closely sharing their lives. Steve has also just visited this island, and he enjoys immersing in nature and being away from the city.

Steve seems to be the antithesis of the typical expat. Moving to a new school, he now finds himself in the company of many foreigners teaching ESL. Steve explains, "In my first school, there were only one or two of us foreigners. Now in my new job, there is a staff room of Westerners. I'm thinking, wow these guys are really loud. They're so noisy."

Most ESL teachers take on the job to get a chance to live abroad and see the world. "A lot of teachers in my school come and go, living the backpacker kind of lifestyle. They come from America, Canada, South Africa, Australia, New Zealand, and England. He explains, "Some of them are just doing it because they are quite young. So it's just part of their overseas experience. And there are a few who do it for a professional career."

So now, Steve faces reverse culture shock. The international group teachers often gather together for barbecues. But this homebody prefers to skip the weekend socials with his co-teachers. Steve sighs, "I tend to stay away from that. I've spent all week at work, the last thing I want to do is spend more time with them. There are about 15 of us expats teaching ESL."

Even the student make-up in his current school differs greatly from his previous teaching experience. In the business school near Bugis, Steve used to teach students from everywhere. He shares, "The students were from overseas, mostly China, Korea, some from Indonesia, Malaysia, a few from the Philippines, Mongolia, and also quite a number from Sri Lanka and India."

He appreciated the mix of cultures. And coming from different countries and speaking different languages, they were forced to speak English to each other. Now, he is faced with a dominantly Chinese student population learning English. "My current school has 80 percent Chinese students." Probing deeper on who these students are, he then explains to me. "Their families are based in China. Their average age is 22 to 23 and most of them are just out of university. It's a private school which focuses mainly on business programmes. In fact, the main income earner for the school is the post-graduate business degrees."

Baffled why they would choose to come to Singapore, he further elaborates, "There are various reasons why they are here. Some of them want to go into business. For some, they see English as a stepping-stone for their graduate classes. Some are here for holiday. Their parents send them here for one or two months." I ask if there is a fixed school term and he shakes his head. "No, we get new students every day. And it's tough, it's the McDonald's of English learning."

But the shocking revelation for me is that a good number of his students are not really interested to learn how to speak English. He shares about the phenomenon of the "Study Mamas". "Because our school is located close to Geylang, we get a number of "working students". They work at night." Geylang is an area in the eastern section of Singapore known for brothels and where prostitutes roam freely at night. Steve sheds light on the grim reality of the study mamas: "Getting a student visa means they can stay in the country for a long time. That's their way to stay here. But you can pretty much tell, these are the students who take the afternoon classes. They choose classes later in the day. Obviously, they are too tired to wake up early in the morning. We call them C Classes. No one really likes to do the C Classes. I did it once when I joined the school and I told my boss that I couldn't do it anymore."

He tells me that many of them are young girls from China. They don't really want to learn English, but they are required to show up for attendance to stay in school. To conform to the rule, he confides, "Many of them would show up and leave the room as soon as I have taken their attendance."

After nearly six years since his move to Singapore in July 2003, the honeymoon period is clearly over for Steve. He does get annoyed with the blaring music coming out of mobile phones in the MRT. He has seen one too many fights in the MRT, where a lady pushes another, a fight ensues, and the entire train just watches. Steve comments, "They don't want to get involved." When a German foreigner started talking to him in the MRT, other passengers eavesdropped. They were bemused at the concept of striking a conversation with a total stranger.

Living here for many years, Steve decided to apply for his Permanent Residency. After the fourth try, it was finally approved. He shares with me some of his favorites spots in his adopted country, "The Swissotel's top floor has the best view on New Year's Eve. You get a 360 degree view of Singapore." For an indulgence on special occasions, he suggests heading to the Raffles Hotel, where he ate a special meal on his 30th birthday. To get away from the maddening city life, there's Pulau Ubin and the boardwalk along Changi Beach. For stocking up on fine cheeses, salami, and wines, there's Jones in Dempsey Hill.

But the biggest discovery, Steve realizes, is that perhaps it is time to take a break of six months or so from Singapore. The routine is just getting to him. With his shoulders slouched down and a serious look on his face, he tells me, "Everyday feels the same. The sun rises at the same time. It sets at the same time. You get the same feeling at the MRT or bus. Life is easy. And perhaps, it is too easy." The predictability and the routine has become drudgery for Steve.

This mild-mannered guy got the shock of his life when one day he snapped at the grumpy cashier in the grocery, asking her "Are you angry?" He was just frustrated. But he was shocked at the person he had become when he started telling people off.

Steve cannot pursue his passion for long drives here, as he would in New Zealand. Neither can he go fishing. As a serious angler in New Zealand, he is accustomed to catching big fish. He does not attempt to fish in Changi Beach or other spots in Singapore as he has noticed that the anglers rarely seem to catch any fish there, and even if they do, Steve thinks they are too small. It is definitely not the fishing he is accustomed to.

It all starts to add up for me. A life of all work and no play, with no sick leave or holidays over an extended period of time will definitely make any person angry and frustrated. It pushes one to his limit. And no matter how meek or mild you are, with no work-life balance, even the gentlest lamb can roar into a lion, in Steve's case, a feisty Merlion.

15 *In Pursuit of Happiness*

Margaret Flink, American
40 years old, International School Science Teacher,
Moved to Singapore in July 2007

How We Met

The night scene in Singapore has its cliché places where you are bound to find expats. There is Clarke Quay, set by the Singapore River, and its abundant bar and restaurant offerings. You can have anything you want here, from Chinese food to Italian food, and you can have your drink anyway you want it too. Do you want to dance in the Pump Room, or do you prefer pretending to be a sick patient in The Clinic, complete with wheelchairs and hospital beds?

Then there is Holland Village, more relaxed than Clarke Quay, close to the residential area of choice of many expatriates. Restaurants abound here as well. There is also Emerald Hill, a side street filled with quaint bars and restaurants located in vibrantly restored shophouses. New to Singapore, my flatmate and I, with some of her co-teachers, met up one Friday night at Emerald Hill in September 2007.

One of my flatmate's friends is Margaret, whom I met in Que Pasa that night. Drinking some beers and laughing, she definitely appeared fashionable together with her best friend Yada, both clad in cute Bebe outfits. These two girls were obviously the life of the party, just being crazy with their fellow teachers from the Overseas Family School. But Margaret excused herself early in the night to head home as she had to get up early for her yoga class the next day. That night Margaret was beaming with pride, telling her co-teachers that her students posted a video of her dissecting a frog on YouTube. Margaret is called "Miss Flink", teaching science to middle school students.

Her Story

It was Saturday morning. My alarm rang at 6 am. I rolled out of bed for an early morning date with Margaret Flink, in time for the first Bikram Yoga class scheduled for the day at 8 am. She calls it her date with the gas chamber.

We agreed to meet at 7:40 am. With the sky barely breaking into light, I headed to the MRT in City Hall. Bright and chipper in a vibrant red blouse, she was standing by the taxi stand of Raffles City waiting for me. We headed up to the Bikram Yoga Studio on the second floor, where other fellow morning people were already waiting for the class to start. Everyone knew Margaret here, from the instructors, to the receptionists, and fellow classmates.

We headed to the locker room where we undressed to a bare minimum of sports bra and shorts. Margaret revealed an amazing body with well-sculpted muscles on her arms, legs, thighs, and abs. A number of expats and Singaporeans filed into the locker room and the friendly vibe was tangible, as there was a friendly exchange of smiles and pleasant conversation. Everyone seemed happy.

I sat in the 40°C room and tried to get my body acquainted with the heat. But as the minutes went by, the heat seemed to intensify. A young petite Singaporean lady came in—Eleanor, the yoga instructor. She stood on the stage, first introducing me as the new student to the class, then instructing us with the detailed step-by-step process on what to do for each pose. Her voice was pleasant, but fast and motivating. Perhaps it was too early in the morning, but I couldn't figure out what she was saying. She lost me at "cock" something. For every pose, she identified what it was good for, such as it being beneficial for digestion, improving metabolism, or the spleen, etc.

With a class of three men and 17 women, it was a pretty good turnout for 8 am on a Saturday morning. Margaret stood in front of me. She had been doing Bikram for over three years now and she had done it consecutively every single day for the past 49 days. She was aiming for 75 days straight, breaking it only when her parents arrive in late March for a visit.

Knowing she was a model student, I had my eyes fixated on Margaret's every move. I could hear myself thinking, "I would like to look as amazing as Margaret does in my 40s." Then I realized, "Heck, I wouldn't mind looking the way she does, now in my thirties."

As the heat intensified, so did the poses. The *savasana*, the lying pose, was always a joy. I stared at the clock. It said 8:40 am. And it was quite a feat to make it this far. My teacher then said that it was just the warm up, now the real workout would begin.

"Is she serious?" I silently thought to myself. I gasped and wondered if I could endure another 50 minutes of this. All Bikram classes are an hour-and-a-half long. By 9 am, my tummy was growling and begging for breakfast. The image of rosti (grated and fried potato patties) with sour cream and a pork sausage in Marche—a Swiss restaurant in Vivo City and my favorite brunch place with food stations serving everything from crepes, paella, to chocolate mousse—began to linger in my head.

The instructor thanked us not just for coming, but also for the privilege of doing the practice with her. She then ended the session with hands clasp together, saying "Namaste!" After the workout and a few minutes of meditation, my classmates congratulated me on surviving my first class. I showered, immersed in a sense of accomplishment at being up and completing a rigorous yoga class by 10 am on a Saturday morning. After that, Margaret and I headed down to the basement of Raffles City for a drink of fresh apple wheatgrass juice before embarking on our MRT ride to Vivo City.

She spoke in fluent Mandarin to the auntie selling the freshly squeezed juices, and they greeted her like a long lost friend. Smiles everywhere. She explained to me in English what they had just said, "You have many friends!" Margaret shed light on her bond with the aunties, "I come here after every yoga class, sometimes they make me sit on the stool while waiting for my drink to be prepared. Or after one glass, I sit there (pointing to the stool) until they make me a second glass."

At this point, this Mexican-Swiss American science teacher had already successfully charmed me. She definitely exudes a positive energy, and just being around her makes people happy. I marvel at how she connects with people from the Chinese aunties making her juice to little kids walking by. She makes eye contact with strangers and smiles at everyone. She's almost like a mascot. Here in Singapore where smiles and warm, friendly people are scarce, Margaret's sunny personality is definitely a breath of fresh air.

This spunky science teacher moved to Singapore in July 2007. But prior to that, she had 10 years of experience teaching in Columbia, West Africa, Perth (Australia), Shanghai (China), and several cities in the United States.

Everyone calls Singapore "Asia Lite", and Margaret could not agree more. It is clean and easy. After a divorce from her husband, she needed a change of scene from the small population of Washington State. She moved to Florida with her fellow teacher and close friend Yada. Ready for a change, Yada, Yada's cousin Soleil, and Margaret all applied for teaching jobs in Singapore. Fortunately, they all obtained teaching positions in the Overseas Family School (OFS). The transition to the school and Singapore was made even easier having former colleagues in Shanghai working in the same school.

A seasoned international schoolteacher and a survivor of three bouts of malaria, moving to Singapore was a breeze. It was definitely more cosmopolitan than her previous international postings. Finding an apartment was also much easier than in the other cities she had lived in. For some of her colleagues on their first foreign posting, finding a condominium was a bit of challenge. The school provided a real estate agent to show them possible rentals. Knowing her needs as single woman, she told the agent, "Look at us. We're single. You think we want to live in a place called Plantation? Do you see any husband or kids? Let's move... bring us closer to the center of the city."

Work-wise, teaching at Overseas Family School has been a joy. Margaret could easily have chosen to work in the American school, but she revels in the diversity this school brings. The team of eleven in the science department comes from all over the world. They bring in different techniques and experiences that have worked in other countries, providing fresh ways to teach their lessons. Her eyes light up as she tells me, "One teacher says, 'where I'm from we teach it this way.' Another teacher says, 'where I'm from we teach it that way' Oh my gosh, that's so cool! I like that. We put it together to create the best way or method to teach our concepts."

But her real joy is teaching such a diverse mix of students from all around the world. She beams a big smile, "They're from everywhere. It's weird, sometimes I get caught up in normal everyday teaching. Then I look at them, you're from India, you're from Saudi Arabia, you're from Scotland, and you're arguing just like brothers and sisters about where to put the test tubes on the retort stand." I ask where her students are from, "There are a few Singaporeans. But most of them are South African, Australian, Kiwi, from the Philippines, Chile, America…" Add to that the international mix of teachers, bringing with them a wealth of overseas travel and work experience from the varied countries they've lived in. Margaret absolutely loves this, what she aptly calls "My little global society".

As we dig into our brunch, I have a plate of rosti and garlic sausage, while Margaret chooses a savory crepe. Put two single girls together and it won't be long before you share battle scars from the tough world of dating. A year and a half ago, Margaret and her friends would describe Singapore as a drought. These three American single ladies rarely spotted good-looking men in town. So when they did, they called it a rainfall. Margaret was then into the Clarke Quay scene, frequenting The Pump Room and dating all sorts of characters she met there.

When I had first met Margaret, she was still enjoying the colorful nightlife in Clarke Quay. She frequented the Pump Room. Her vivacious personality and natural Latina vibe easily attracted a number of men. But this is now a thing of the past. Instead of frequently going out at night, she spends more time reading spiritual book by Wayne Dyer, Byron Katie, and Eckhart Toelle.

Before me now is a more serene, centered, happy, and confident woman. She no longer frequents the club scene, but occasionally dates interesting men she meets on an Internet dating site. She keeps an open mind in meeting people from different races and backgrounds. Many people have told me it is more difficult for a Caucasian single girl in Singapore to date than it is for an Asian woman. Caucasian men are attracted to Asian women. But for some reason, you see few Asian men with Caucasian women.

Margaret tells me that she has dated a few Singaporean men. For many of them, she was the first Caucasian woman they had dated and they enjoyed the novelty of it. She says, "A lot of times, they think it's really cool to go out with a white girl. It's so exciting for them. I'm not "Me! Me!". Neither does she require the guys to carry her handbag, as we both have noticed many Asian women expect their boyfriends to do. But later on the men became very clingy. One guy got very upset when she did not pick up her phone when he called. She gently explained that she turns her phone on silent when she is out for lunch with a friend and he demanded that she should answer the phone when he calls.

After dating another guy for a week, he started talking about marriage. He plotted a date with her involving going to his three-year-old niece's birthday party, dinner, housewarming party to meet his parents, then finally a movie at 1 am. The wise teacher immediately said thanks and goodbye to this guy as well.

Another guy probed if there were guys with her when she went out with colleagues. She answered, "Yes, I guess there was a guy." Enraged he probed further, "You don't remember you were with a guy?" Margaret explains "I was a group of people, and there was a guy there." Exasperated she tells him, "I've been dating you for two weeks, you should know by now that I'm dating you, not a 26-year-old guy who happens to be with our group."

One clingy guy asked where she was, or why she wasn't answering his call at 2 am. She answered the next day, "I was asleep naturally."

Margaret notes how meticulously clean Singaporean men are. One guy she dated showed up driving his car wearing white gloves. I asked what car he was driving, thinking it was an expensive Jaguar. "A Honda Civic!" she said. But he assured her it was pretty special, "It was turbo!" We both burst into contagious laughter. This gloved date was the same guy who struggled to maneuver his car out of her carpark. The same guy freaked out and refused to get out of his car when he saw a small lizard. The science teacher was not at all impressed.

Despite the series of dating disasters, Margaret remains unfazed. She does not cling to men, nor does she let clingy men into her life. I tell her of the marked difference in the Margaret of many months past and this woman before me, and she confides, "I'm more accepting now." She is done with the pastime of many single women—waiting, wondering, and second-guessing why a guy didn't call again. "I'm so done with that," she states as a matter of fact. Just like the message of the movie and her favorite book *He's Just Not That Into You*, there are no excuses. I share a lesson my mother planted into my head when I was in my early twenties, "Being busy is not an excuse for a guy not to call. No guy is too busy, unless he is a soldier at war and crawling in the ground, dodging bullets. A guy has time to call if he likes you." Margaret bursts into a long, spirited laughter, marveling and agreeing with my mother's wise words.

For almost a year now, she has been on a path to taking better care of herself on a physical, emotional, and spiritual level. She does not spend her time waiting for phone calls from men, or getting involved in toxic relationships. Instead, she indulges in a lot of alone time, reading, meditating. Practicing yoga religiously is important for Margaret, for it is a way of being kind to her body, which serves her well everyday. It calms and centers her, she explains: "It's my meditation. For a hour and a half, someone's telling me what to do." It is helping her love herself more. "I'm starting to connect with my body. I'm being a lot easier on my body now. I like my body and I treat my body well."

As a teacher who spends most of her days attending to the 11- to 14-year-old children and telling them how amazing they are, she finds it important to nourish herself too. She wakes up on some days, excited at the thought of having a date with herself. She teaches me, "Why not? Here we are telling people that they're amazing, they're so precious. We have to do that to ourselves in order to be able to do that better for other people."

Margaret is happy in her own company, and focuses on improving her health and well-being. She enjoys spending time by herself. She even finds much joy with the bats, geckos and birds who pay her a visit in her apartment, seeing this as the silver lining to living in her apartment, which is not easily accessible.

She happily takes the cab and the MRT. She too has her share of chatty cab drivers who often misinterpret her sunny personality. She narrates her cab nightmare, "One time I acted like I was calling the police, 'this cab is taking two wrong turns, and I have no idea where he is taking me'…The cab driver immediately said, 'No, no… I take you right way.' I tell him, 'You're being weird uncle. You need to take me home now, or I'm telling this police car where we are right now.'" She later tells me that the cab driver initially said weird thing like, "Oh you have a lover, would you like me to be your lover?" She explains that they are not used to single girls being friendly. On another occasion, she threatened the driver, "I've dialed 9-9, if you don't take me home right away, I will dial the last nine and call the police." Luckily, she has always arrived home unharmed. But she has learned not to be too chatty with the cab drivers, and to use the time in the cab to call her parents in the US instead.

Seeing that she is such a trendy girl, I ask how she enjoys shopping in Singapore. At the edge of my seat, hoping for some great shopping tips, I am surprised that she does not enjoy shopping here. "The clothes don't fit me right." Margaret states. Her curvy Latina figure doesn't fit well with the Asian clothes. She even notices that she has more muscle than many Asian men. But this sweet lady isn't complaining. It just is.

Very close to her parents, her adorable Mexican mother and her Swiss father come to visit every year. Coming from a small American town in Seattle, Washington, they were initially overwhelmed by the diversity of the cultures in Singapore. The sights, sounds, and smells of the hawker centers were initially overwhelming. But it is this very diversity that Margaret loves, a blend of Chinese, Malay, Indian, and other Asian cultures. Never mind if she sometimes finds herself in awkward situations. One day she was looking for costumes in Arab Street. Famished, she entered a restaurant. Only men were dining. They all stared at her and became silent when she ordered her kebab. The man at the counter said, "No more kebab." She saw everyone else had a kebab, and a guy was just served kebab. She asked again. "I'm telling you no more kebab," he sternly answered. With all eyes on her, this spunky chick managed to have her last say, "Well, that's just rude", then quickly walked away from the awkward situation.

Focused on her work, her practice of yoga, studying for a teaching certification exam, and enriching herself with good spiritual books, Margaret truly lives a well-rounded life. Weekends start off with her early morning Bikram yoga class at 8 am, brunch with friends at Marche in Vivo City, and checking a hundred exam papers. But doing all things in moderation, she makes time for the monthly kickball game with a bunch of expat friends in Little India.

Aware that her two-year teaching contract at OFS is about to be up, and it would be another opportunity to move on to another city, I ask Margaret of her plans. "My ultimate dream is to go back to Africa. I'd like to go with somebody. I'd like to be married and go back, because being a single woman in Africa is very difficult. I'd like to take care of animals or baby with AIDS. There are a lot of orphans there, with no parents because their parents have died of AIDS. I'd like to get recharged and healed, get married, then maybe Singapore can be my base." In the meantime, she is focusing all her attention and energy on recharging her batteries.

Friends have told her it would take a really special man to be with her. I cannot agree more, for she deserves nothing less than that. Someone with so much intelligence and an infectious, positive energy deserves nothing more. Whoever the man is will be lucky to be filled with such a positive presence in his life. With heaps of grading awaiting her, we bid each other goodbye. As I walk away, I feel a bounce to my step. My batteries have been recharged by the early morning yoga, the nourishing brunch, and the healthy conversation. She has generously given me a glimpse of her path to happiness, and I have already become richer by the experience.

16 *Living by the Seasons*

Guillaume Paupy, French
36 years old, Director of Food & Beverage, Four Seasons Hotel Singapore
Moved to Singapore in November 2008, Married with two kids

How We Met

Working as a food and travel writer, my job requires me to keep abreast of the latest news from hotels and restaurants regarding new dishes, food festivals and offerings for Mother's Days, Father's Day, and other big holidays for dining out and so on. In the process, the hotels foster cordial relations with media people like me. At the end of the year, many hotels hold a Christmas party for the media, such as the Four Seasons Hotel which invited me to a masquerade party in early December. The invite stated that we should come in a mask.

Having grown weary of being a single woman thrust into a roomful of strangers at these social events, I asked if I could bring a companion. They gladly honored my request. My dearest friend Emmanuel and accomplice to this event enthusiastically provided two gorgeous gold and green masks he asked a friend to send over from Manila. But my dear date was coming in from a work meeting in Jakarta. His flight arrived late, forcing me to attend the event alone. Dressed in a flattering little black dress, I arrived at the Four Seasons looking glamorous. Fiddling with my mask and my name cards, I was met by the big shots from the hotel. My Spanish sounding surname was instantly a hit with the Spanish GM. After the necessary introductions, I found myself standing alone. Then a handsome French man approached me. His dark brown hair, tall built, and boyish features all reminded me of my Belgian ex-boyfriend. But this guy seemed ten times more charming than my ex. It was difficult to decipher whether it was bitterness from the break-up or this man's distinctly French accent that caused me to arrive at that immediate conclusion.

He introduced himself as Guillaume Paupy. We exchanged our cards in the formal Singapore fashion, presenting it with both left and right hands holding the base of the card. His name card stated his position as "Director of Food & Beverage". He read my name card, noting me as the author of the book *Do's and Don'ts in the Philippines*. We instantly connected, and it wasn't long before we were both lost in an animated conversation about my beautiful Philippine islands. Married to a Brazilian woman, he seemed to be badly bitten by a love affair for the tropics. He told me he had just returned to Singapore a little over a month back. But this is his second stint in Singapore, as he was assigned here with a different hotel a few years ago.

A Frenchman married to a Brazilian and now beginning his second stint in Singapore is certain to be an interesting subject for this book. We kept in touch. I shared some of my photographs and articles on the Philippines on my websites, and Guallaume was definitely smitten by my archipelago. He promised to visit the beaches.

His Story

Now in my early thirties, my body is no longer as forgiving. Since I moved to Singapore, I have succumbed to eating more carbohydrates. The plates of *char kway teow*, duck noodles, chicken rice, and blueberry fluff from BreadTalk have happily parked themselves on my belly. I often rubbed my belly gently, feeling very much like a kangaroo carrying a joey. In anticipation of my sister's upcoming wedding, I desperately needed to shed off my protruding pouch. I did phase 1 of the South Beach diet, where I had to give up sugar, fruits, carbohydrates, caffeine and alcohol strictly for two weeks. This was a real challenge in Singapore, more so for a food writer like me.

I suffered much withdrawals and a severe migraine on the first day, but with much determination I survived nine days of this diet. On my tenth day, I was to have lunch with Guallaume at the Four Seasons Hotel. Dining at the Four Seasons is no everyday affair, and the temptation to break my diet was so immense.

Dressed in a chic black dress and spunky red heels, I was torn between breaking a sweat on the MRT or the cool yet pricy cab to get to the hotel. I opted for the cab only to be misunderstood by the driver, taking me to "Season's Park" condominium instead of the Four Seasons hotel.

I called Guillaume on my mobile phone as soon as I arrived at the hotel lobby. In Singapore, where people arrive promptly at the appointed time, I apologized profusely for being a few minutes late. But he told me not to worry. He arrived in the lobby, looking smart in his perfectly crisp black suit. In his thick French accent, he asked what I wanted for lunch. Telling him of my no-carb diet, I conveyed my wish for a healthy meal. We then walked up the grand staircase to Jiang-Nan Chun, the Cantonese restaurant on the second floor of the hotel. A table was awaiting us in a quiet section of the restaurant, away from the other guests. I asked him how to say his name properly. He said "Gee-yom". It's the French version of William, but people often can't pronounce it. He said, "You can call me G, GP, but not Bill."

Dining with the hotel's F&B Director has its perks. You are sure to get superior service. The wait staff was extra courteous and attentive. Chef Benjamin Ng greeted Guillaume and he conveyed my special dietary request. My hyperactive mind was briefly polluted with thoughts of carb-loaded Chinese standards like crispy noodles and fried rice. But the talented chef prepared a wonderful meal with minimal carbohydrates consisting of a *dim sum* platter, an unforgettable melt-in-your-mouth steamed cod in soy, shitake mushroom and other fungi steamed in paper, and another dish of sautéed greens with garlic.

The French people are known for their flair for living the good life. They are noted for their fashion style, their deep love affair for fine food, and other indulgencese. But what makes it so remarkable is how effortlessly they execute their decadent lifestyle, and in the end they remain slim and healthy. Looking frumpy and dressing scruffily is not acceptable in France. But neither is dieting and going to the gym. It remains a mystery how they do it. Hence books like Mireille Guiliano's *Why French Women Don't Get Fat* and Helena Frith Powell's *Two Lipsticks and A Lover* give other women from around the world a glimpse of how to live a good life and still look smashing like the French women do.

As I conversed with Guillaume, I realized I could have saved myself a few bucks by just spending time with this French man instead of buying those books. As we talked, he revealed not only a colorful life of a hotelier, but he was also imparting valuable lessons in living well as the French do.

At the young age of 36, this hotelier had lived in the most unusual countries. When he left Paris at 20, he thought, "Paris is finished for me. I'm going to travel the whole world. I will get married when I am 45." So the young Guallaume went to Switzerland to study for three years. He then began his hotel career in Tunisia. A most unusual destination to embark on a hotel career, I thought. But I was aware that Tunisia is one of the next big travel destinations as I had written a small feature on it in Silver Kris' travel magazine about a year ago. He tells me about Tunisia, "I loved it. I loved the country. The messier the country, the more I like it. Just don't put me in the war."

After a year working in Tunisia, he continued his adventure in Guatemala. His plans to remain single and remain committed to his demanding job as an expat in the hotel industry until he reached 45 immediately fizzled out. He fell in love with Fernanda, a Brazilian lady. But he also fell deeply in love with Guatemala. He describes it as "one of the best country I lived in". Abundant in natural beauty, he says, "Nature there is beautiful. And every weekend you can see a lot of things. It has a very rich culture. They have the Maya ruins. You can rent a car and you can travel to Belize, the Carribean, and all over Central America. We reached Panama. The country is so small, in two days you already have a big trip." He cannot put to words how rich and gorgeous the country is, called a biodiversity hotspot for its abundant natural offerings.

Together with his wife, his foreign postings continued in more exotic destinations. Next stop was Lebanon, which he describes as "fantastic". He tells me there are many people speaking French and

English here. "There are many French people from Paris there. We say it is an extension of Paris." What he loves best is the people, "I never saw people having so much fun. People are always out, always drinking, eating, and smoking."

His wife is half-Brazilian and half-Lebanese. For her, being there was a way of connecting to her father's relatives. GP remembers this phase in his life, "But my wife didn't like it because it was a war country. Every six months, Israel attacked. It was very scary." After a year, they moved to the northeast coast of Brazil called Salvador da Baia. He describes it to be where the slaves from Africa lived, and it has a Carribean vibe. It is a very, very old town, which is beautiful architecturally and very rich culturally. There are a lot of mulattos living there. "It is fantastic, the weather, the light is beautiful. It is a resort town." It was idyllic for the Frenchman and his wife. They have already bought a plot of land there for their retirement years. His mom and his grandmother have fallen in love with the place too, and have left their beloved France and moved there to retire as well.

He then worked in Tokyo for three years, where he was fascinated with the bustling city's unparalleled energy. He tells me. "You know you can see everything on TV, so you're not surprised anymore. But when you arrive in Tokyo, wow! You just have to go there and live it." The architecture, the music, the culture, the excellent service and the people were all amazing for this well-traveled hotelier. And unlike what we learn in schools that the Japanese work long hours, GP tells me, "Everybody thinks they work more in Tokyo than anywhere in the world. Yes, they work many hours, but they have so many holidays."

He then had a two-year stint in Singapore, before spending many months in his beloved wife's Brazil. He has obviously taken on the vibrant spirit of the Brazilians as he laments how he is sad to miss the Carnival this year. As much as he loves living in Brazil, a hotelier's job inherently requires him to move to a new country every few years. GP explains that it is not only demanding for him, but also requires much sacrifice for his wife. "It's very hard to marry a hotelier. You have to give your life to the hotel. It's a business that is open 24 hours. You move so fast, and your wife does not have the time to find a job or make friends. She must be very much in love with her husband."

The decision to move back to Singapore was not only a career decision for Guillaume to be in the regional hub of the Four Seasons, but also a personal decision for his family. He elaborates, "I've been married for ten years now. My wife was willing to come back to Asia only if it was Singapore. She was very excited to come back here because she has a lot of friends and it is the easiest place to live in."

Guillaume and his wife have two adorable little girls aged two and four. Upon his return, he noticed how much Singapore has changed since he left in 2006. "Singapore has changed a lot in two years. There is much more construction and new buildings coming up, price have also increased." But the most notable difference for him, "People drink different wines—that's a big difference for me." Only a French man and a serious wine connoisseur would notice such a change, I probe him deeper on his observation. Is it better or worse I ask?

Definitely better, he tells me. "They used to drink a lot of heavy wines like Shiraz from Australia." I comment how his bold wines are not suitable for the hot humid days in Singapore. "Absolutely!" he agrees. Noting the improvement, he reports, "Now, they are drinking different wines, South American wines."

As we eat the *dim sum* combination consisting of chicken pastry with black pepper sauce and mushroom, crab dumpling, steamed *siew mai*, and chicken dumpling with crab meat on top, he tells me not to eat the flaky pastry to honor my carb-free diet.

His life in Singapore as a family man and hotelier is very stable and easy. He lives in Balmoral Park, a mere five-minute walk to his hotel on Orchard. Because of his stint in Tokyo, he has learned the ease of getting around on a bike. He cycles to and from work, this way he gets some exercise. It is also his clever solution to the humidity. "You can live 50 meters away from work. But you cross the street and you are sweaty." So his solution is to cycle to work, then shower when he gets to the hotel.

When I ask if he has taken the MRT, he tells me he never takes it. His wife has a car to take the kids around. Curious, he asks me and the waiter refilling our tea cups, "Tell me, what happens in the MRT?" The young waiter then goes on to narrate how some people randomly take photos of total strangers on their phones on the train. He tells us that it has happened thrice to his girlfriend. Perhaps his girlfriend is pretty, GP and I say out loud. "No, my girlfriend is not pretty." The Frenchman is shocked that the young boy would admit his girlfriend is not much of a looker.

Guillaume tells me many people have asked to take photos with his two daughters. With the lovely mix of French and Brazilian features, I can imagine how adorable they are. Linking up with GP later on Facebook, I see his profile photo with his two little angels. The blend of two cultures couldn't have been a better match.

His life is devoted to his work and his family. Saturdays are spent going to the market near Balestier Road with his two little ones. He shops for fresh fruits and vegetables, and cooks for his family on weekends. He religiously partakes of Loy Kee Best Chicken Rice close to the market. I ask how he likes hawker cuisine. He admits that apart from chicken rice, he cannot take spices. "I can't take spicy food. For French people, when you put some spices on food, it is because the food is really bad. When the food is fresh, you eat it the way it is. The more sauce you put, the more you are masking its freshness. The fresher it is, the better."

The French live by the seasons. They cook and eat fruits and vegetables that are in their prime, celebrating the importance of seasonal eating.

I ask if he is surprised that people don't cook here. "Not at all," he says. "It's so convenient to go down and eat at a hawker. Imagine if we have that in Europe, all your friends having good food, why will you bother cooking everyday? I'm not surprised."

Apart from the market, the family loves going to Sentosa on Saturday evenings from 4 to 6 pm. The kids love the zoo. He tells me, "The Singapore Zoo is like Disneyland. You're in close contact with the animals. It's beautiful. It's like having lunch in an open kitchen." The family likes the Bird Park too, especially the sight of all the colorful birds everywhere.

Aside from the safety and the ease, Guallaume agrees that everything is available in Singapore. Well, almost everything. He has tried all the bakeries in search of good bread. But to his dismay, it looks like importing bread from the US or France may be the solution in obtaining the finest quality crusty bread to meet his high standards for his discerning hotel guests. This French gourmand tells me the humid conditions make it not ideal, "You can't find good bread in Singapore. It's so wet. You buy bread and an hour after, it's a piece of rubber."

He agrees that Singapore is a shopping paradise with many options. But going to the mall in Singapore is very different from his experience of shopping in Paris. "In my family, I'm always surrounded by a lot of women, my sister, mother, grandmother, and they used to drag me to shop in Paris on Saturdays. The good thing is you don't get bored because Parisian shopping is not in malls but in shops along the streets." He explains "You visit the shops and at the same time you are getting to know Paris. You go into a shop, and then you stop and have a coffee. You pop into another shop and then you have your lunch at a nearby restaurant." It is very different from the mall culture instilled in Singaporean life. He continues, "Here it's really a pain to go shopping. You find every thing inside the mall, yes. But there is nothing charming about it."

For this classy Parisian, there is joy in the adventure of finding something special. He tells me how he found a little shop in Sims Avenue in Geylang selling lovely blue and white pots imported from China. So far that is the only precious shopping adventure he has had in Singapore.

Our meal unfolds in a perfect pace. We partake of each dish with enthusiam, engaging in conversation between bites. The chef appears as we work on our fourth course, sautéed greens. The meal is light yet satisfying. GP tells the Chinese chef that he wants a different dessert. He liked the aloe vera served to him before and found it refreshing, but he wants to try something new.

An unusual banana fritter wrapped in a shredded fillo pastry and served with vanilla ice cream finally succeeds in tempting me. Taking a cue from the French, any woman in my situation would definitely have this dessert. So I break my diet, with little trace of guilt or remorse. And it is delicious. I do not finish my scoop of ice cream, but I watch as Guillaume savors every bit of his ice cream.

For a hotelier who seeks messy, challenging postings, perhaps Singapore is not an ideal match for him. He tells me he is happy with the efficiency at work, although he misses the energy and creativity he had experienced in Brazil. He marvels at their ingenuity, citing eco-friendly solutions the Brazilians have created. But right now in this season in his life and career, Singapore is the right place for him.

We are both satisfied with our healthy meal. I marvel at how joyfully I have honored my diet (well for the most part), learning as the French would how to eat in a healthy but delicious way. Guillaume is content with his meal too. He tells me, "The French say you have to leave the table still a little hungry. If you eat too much, it is not good."

I believe this expat too has been following this with the seasons in his life. He leaves each country he is assigned to still feeling a little hungry. This way his experiences remain fresh and pertinent to the season in his life. These for me are wise lessons we can learn from the French.

17 *Tai Tais: Women Who Lunch*

Four Thai women, Mani*, Ruam, Gift and Jo

How We Met

About four months ago, my friend Shawn invited me to his cast party's barbecue. He sent me a message on my phone telling me to head to Mt. Pleasant. For some reason, I imagined wooden picnic benches amidst verdant greens. Instead, the cab driver drove into a long driveway. The property seemed like a compound, but inside it was a gorgeous commanding black and white colonial house. It had high ceilings, large windows, and a Thai decoration. Outside was a large garden, big enough to be a park and playground in some of the smaller towns in Singapore. There too was a thatched hut and a swimming pool. It felt very much like a tropical resort.

Laid out on a table was a most delectable spread of food including Korean *chapchae* (glass noodles), *tom yum goong*, sticky rice, Thai salads, and numerous Thai dishes I had never seen before. The cast of the documentary by filmmaker Sherman Ong had a merry mix of Japanese, Thai, Filipino, Korean, and Indonesians. All the cast members sat around dining alfresco. Near the grill with seafood and sausages were a group of Caucasian men holding their glasses of wine and engrossed in conversation. And sitting comfortably on a set of wicker chairs were a group of Thai women, looking after their adorable toddlers. Their cute little faces captured the lovely blend of Caucasian and Asian features, making it impossible not to fall in love with them.

Mani, the owner of the house, was a gorgeous woman in her thirties. Tall and dressed in a summery white loose blouse with fair white skin and a very pleasant face, it was not a surprise to learn that she was a model. She had invited another model, a young, very slim Chinese lady with bangs covering her forehead, wearing a sexy black top. Mani later brought down her portfolio of headshots, magazine, and advertising work from her days working as a model in Thailand, Singapore, and other parts of the world.

There were ten little children running around and playing. They would stop and get a bite of sticky rice kept in a wicker basket, then go back to whatever game amused them. Some cycled around in a small tricycle, while others ran around. I played with some kids and later got to know their Thai mums. I met Ruam, a hands-on mum of three kids, a eight-year-old daughter, a six-year-old son, and the littlest one, one and a half-year-old Matthew, who would never be far away from his mum.

Being a food writer, I was most definitely intrigued by the food. All the Thai food served was cooked by one of Mani's friend. And Ruam told me that these bunch of mums frequently gathered together to eat their beloved food. Recognizing me as Filipina, Ruam confided that she had lived in the Philippines. Hailing from the Northeastern part of Thailand, she married a New Zealander who had some projects in

Batangas, a provincial city about three hours South of Manila. She was only in her twenties at that time. Leaving home at a young age, she did not know how to cook. That wouldn't have been a problem in Thailand as you can easily purchase good food everywhere, but in Batangas there were no Thai restaurants and getting her spices was difficult. Rawa recounted how she returned home to her mum in tears. She told her mom, "I can't live there. They don't have our food." Tears flowed from her eyes as she ate the fresh cilantro she had long missed. Her wise mother then told her to learn how to cook her favorite dishes. In the true warm Asian hospitality, Ruam invited me to join her friends when they gathered to eat Thai food. It was just all the women minus their husbands.

Having written a hundred-page dissertation on migrant cooking during my graduate studies in Gastronomy, I was aware of the strong power of migrants gathering together and cooking the food of their home country. It made the women feel at ease in the foreign culture by being able not only to partake of food familiar to them, but also to be able to speak in their native tongue. I could not shake off the idea of a plethora of authentic Thai food and a glimpse of the conversations that ensue among these Thai women married to *ang mos*. With one quick call to Mani, she instantly herded her friends and a lunch was set for Monday. The mums were available until 2 pm, for some of them had to fetch their kids from school.

I arrive promptly at noon to an apologetic maid telling me Mani has gone for a swim. A few minutes later, she emerges from her car looking very stylishly pregnant. Wearing a long floral black dress, her bump is now very obvious, unlike the last time I had seen her. She says she is due in a month. Shortly after, her two friends Ruam and Gift arrive with Ruam's son, Matthew, and Gift's one-year-old son and two-year-old daughter. Ruam gives me a peck on both cheeks, as most *ang mohs* greet each other here in Singapore. Mani then comments, "I don't kiss on two cheeks. I just find it too much. Too close." I smile at her, recognizing her sentiment.

The three toddlers, plus Mani's two-year-old daughter Mirabelle, all shriek in seeing each other. These kids play together so often that they already think they are blood relatives. Ruam then settles into a chair, as her son roams around, frequently returning to touch base with his dear mummy. Mani plops herself on the couch and begins applying make-up. I give her a container of freshly baked cookies. Trained well by my mother, I feel awkward going to someone's home without bringing a gift. Knowing they all have kids, I baked a batch of oatmeal chocolate chip cookies, which the kids enjoy immensely, including the very pregnant Mani.

"Were you friends from Thailand?" I ask Mani and Ruam. Mani's energy soars, excited to tell me the story, "I met her in Takashimaya's breastfeeding room." Not being a mum, I am dumbfounded. I am not even aware there is a place to breastfeed in malls. Mani has been modeling since she was 13. Married in her late twenties to a Dutch-American businessman, she moved to Singapore some six years ago. She had been to Singapore countless times before that, working on modeling gigs in the Lion City. During those short stints, she did not make an effort to make any deep friendships. When she moved to Singapore, she still did not have any Thai friends. She found them to be not quite in her league. On one end of the spectrum were Thai prostitutes, and on the other end were mommies. But when she became a mommy two years ago, she realized she wanted to have Thai mommies she could relate with.

During that period, she found herself shopping solo often. And on this day at Takashimaya, at the heart of Orchard Road, she sat in the nursing room breastfeeding three-month-old Mirabelle. There were curtains for the mom's privacy, but when she heard Thai being spoken by another breastfeeding mum, she pulled open the curtain and introduced herself. She was not self-conscious that she was revealing her boobs to this total stranger and fellow countryman. But Ruam, the woman behind the curtain, was shocked by the boldness of this woman. Ruam, a mother of three and resident of Singapore for eight years now, was not in the practice of making friends with strangers in the mall, even if they were Thai. She was skeptical of Mani, this extremely friendly woman all dolled up and put together in chic clothes.

"Even if I know you are Thai, if I see there is no connection, I will not bother talking to you," Ruam stated as a matter of fact. Then after her bold introduction, Mani gave her mobile number and got Ruam's number then quickly headed away. Ruam remained skeptical if this woman would call or sincerely wanted to be friends. She thought it was just one of those things where you exchanged contact numbers and then forgot all about it. But a few days later, Mani and Ruam had dinner. When Ruam introduced her to her other friends who were Thai mothers as well, they were concerned with the model mom's outward appearance. Looking too polished, they imagined she would not have much in common with them. But Ruam looked beyond the model's outward appearance, and saw how deeply Mani cared and loved her daughter. And to this mother of three, her highest priority was being a good mother. She saw her children as the most precious blessings in her life. And she had high respect for others who shared this sentiment.

With her successful friendship with Ruam, Mani now has the habit of picking up other Thai mommies from the supermarket to be her friends. She admits that despite meeting many Thai women at parties, she still finds herself getting along better with the ones she pick up at the grocery store or in the mall.

Ruam is deeply attached to her little Matthew and is savoring every bit of time spent with him. Her eight-year-old daughter Bridget no longer wants to be seen being kissed by her mom in public. She gets embarrassed when her mom kisses her in front of her classmates at school. So now Ruam realizes how quickly kids grow up, making spending time and caring for her kids her top priority.

The animated conversation with these women is a hodge-podge of topics. They start one topic then quickly jump to the next one, with one chiming in to share an anecdote. Mani begins to tell us of her move to Singapore and the contents of her luggage. "I filled my suitcase with food, all food, no clothes. I even brought fish sauce and durian," this model proudly states. During her modeling days here, she did not know there was Golden Mile Complex, a large shopping mall where she could get her Thai staples. But until today, she continues to bring some specialty food like water cockroach, which she can't get in Singapore.

Food and shopping are the top two things the women miss from Thailand. But it helps immensely that there is Golden Mile Complex, which all the three women visit for an authentic Thai meal and to get special ingredients. Ruam says even Tekka Market in Little India carries many of the ingredients they want, with Indian vendors speaking fluent Thai. It helps that Thailand is close by, ensuring access to fresh veggies from their homeland all the time.

Gift now joins the conversation, after getting her son and daughter happily settled with the toys. She chimes in. Even when Gift's mum visits from Hong Kong, she does not care for the usual trip to Chinatown. Instead she insists on going to Golden Mile for her stash of food supplies she can't purchase in Hong Kong. But when you ask them which restaurants there are their favorites, they do not know the names. Instead they tell you to try the beef noodles behind the beauty parlor, for example.

We shift our conversation. I then probe, "Considering Singapore is a shopping mecca for serious shopaholics, you don't like shopping here?" They shake their heads and admit shopping in Bangkok is much better and a tiny fraction of the price of Singapore's offerings. The gorgeous black sundress Mani is wearing looks similar to the dress Penelope Cruz modeled for Mango. But Mani admits that this dress is not a brand name and it only costs equivalent to $17 in Thailand. The three women agree on shopping in JJ Market, as well as Platinum. They advise that it is best to go there with a friend who shares the same fashion sense as you, as you need to buy at least three pieces to get the discounted price. But the youngest in the group, Gift, only 23 years old, says she goes there with her husband. After all, it's so cheap. Even if she buys three pieces, it's still cheaper than buying one piece in Singapore. Ruam, who frequently returns to her hometown in the Northeast Thailand close to the Laos border, says she can buy cheap clothes for a bargain there. "I don't mind paying less for clothes with slashed labels," she says.

We shift from the outdoor sitting area to the dining room of the black and white colonial home and partake of the Thai dishes, whipped up by Mani's two Filipino maids. When asked how often the group gathers, Mani turns to ther trusted maid. The Filipina maid tells me in our native tongue, "Sometimes, they are here up to four times a week."

In front of me is the most amazing spread of Thai food. There are seven dishes including *som tum* (hand pounded papaya salad), *laarb moo* (ground pork salad with fried kaffir lime leaves and chilis), *kao soi gai* (coconut curry broth with chicken) served with rice noodles, green mango slivers with a chili dipping sauce, and dessert of *tako* (a steamed creamy coconut milk with a pandan gelatin base with corn and water chesnut). The little kids again play while eating some sticky rice. The youngest mum, Gift tells me, "Our kids can't get enough of sticky rice." With the kids are happily at play with one another, punctuated by shrieks and tears, the mums are immersed in conversation and tucking into their comfort food.

The women openly lament to me about the difficulty of being a Thai woman in Singapore due to the stereotype of Thai women as prostitutes. All three women are married to *farangs*, the Thai term for a white man. Interestingly, all of them met their husbands before moving to Singapore. And the unique experience of being a mom married to a *farang* is what binds this group of ten women. Their initial meetings were all accidental encounters, which blossomed into looking out and helping each other.

Ruam recounts how she met Gift, the youngest of the group. A Singaporean woman living in Ruam's condominium in Bukit Timah told her about a young Thai lady who was pregnant with her second child while caring for her infant. Ruam immediately became Gift's friend, feeling for the ordeal of being a mom without any help in a foreign country, made more difficult by being pregnant with another child. She often called Gift, cooked for her, ran errands for her, and made sure the young mother was well cared for while her husband was at work.

Gift's husband is a British who spent many years in Thailand and Hongkong. Gift is Thai, but she grew up in Hongkong. She speaks fluent Cantonese, even preferring the ease in reading Cantonese subtitles in movies instead of the longer Thai characters. She calls her life a fairy tale. She says she never imagined herself marrying a foreigner. She was not even attracted to them. But she found a perfect match in her husband, who speaks Thai and Cantonese too.

The glorious joy of eating rice noodles, tightly pressing the sticky rice and pairing it with curries and fresh salads with women who not only share your language and culture, but also life situations, is obviously treasured by these three women. A fourth woman arrives late. Jo is dressed in a corporate outfit. Very enterprising, this ex-banker now runs a small business selling spa products. This enterprising Thai lady lived in London for seven years before moving to Singapore. It was there where she met her British husband.

Each woman has a story to tell of how they had to overcome the stereotype of the Thai sex worker in Singapore. One has a story of being stopped in immigration, with the officers questioning her for several hours and doubting the authenticity of her credit card. They also receive all sorts of comments from cab drivers and rude treatment from waitresses at pubs. All the women agree that there are Thai sex workers in Singapore, but not all Thai women are prostitutes.

The women also complain of the different treatment their husbands receive. Mani tells me how she went to a store four times to get an appliance repaired. Dismayed, she asked her husband to do it instead. In one visit, he was not at all hassled and the necessary repair was done without any problem. Mani is in shock with what her husband can get away with because he is a Caucasian man.

Even his complaint about his running shoes giving him blisters was kindly accommodated by a shoe store, giving him two new pairs until he was finally satisfied. All the women at the table agree that none of us would get away with such a complaint.

They miss their festivals, like the Songkran, the Thai New Year in April. They inform me that it is beyond throwing water at each other as many think it is, but paying respect to the elderly. And despite having temples here, it does not quite feel like home. Yet they continue living their Buddhist faith and way of life.

But while life in Singapore is not perfect, they like it here. For Ruam, she is happy with the education her children are getting at the Canadian school. The parents can be actively involved in school activities, and many students are offsprings of mixed marriages too. Her eight-year-old daughter is excelling in her classes.

Having lived in other countries like Australia and the UK, one thing these women enjoy is the fact that having black hair allows them to blend into this country. They had been referred to as an alien in Australia, making them feel like a strange extraterrestrial creature. Standing out from the crowd, they felt all eyes on them and their black hair. One person even asked Ruam's husband, "Don't you get embarrassed to walk with your Asian wife?" In Singapore, mixed marriages are common. They don't stand out as being too foreign or too different.

But when asked if this is their home, they do not answer yes or no. Mani nicely sums it up, "I can only live in a place with banana trees and coconut trees." Ruam nods in agreement. And while they are in this foreign land, it feels familiar. The tropical heat, access to their herbs, spices, and specialty Thai dishes, and blending in with their black hair makes it feel like home.

Noticing it is two o'clock, Ruam has to leave to fetch her children. The group then quickly disbands and the mums collect their kids. Mani bids them goodbye, without first giving them copies of Thai magazines they share. Again, it makes them feel right at home, away from home.

18 *A Father's Love*

Rom, Filipino
26 years old, Starbucks Barista,
Moved to Singapore in February 2008, Married with two children

How We Met

It is interesting how the world has become so distant. There are people you cross paths with everyday, but it does not necessarily mean you know what they are going through. And you can never assume you know someone. Beyond the happy façade could be an individual going through so much difficulty.

My daily indulgence is having my cup of cappuccino at Starbucks at Raffles City every day. In the process, I have become close to the staff and some of the regulars there. In October 2008, I had already been going to this coffee shop consistently for about six months. I was told that two Filipinos were joining the store's staff: a big burly guy with tattoos named Paul, and a fair-skinned, good-looking guy named Rom. His good looks were hard to ignore, prompting a regular gay customer to immediately ask for his phone number.

It wasn't long before I became buddies with these two baristas. After about three months, Paul left the store. Rom stayed on, excelling as the Assistant Store Manager. Even the baristas working for him enjoyed his professional yet friendly style of management. You could often hear him laughing. And every time he saw me, he would beam a big smile and respectfully call me Ms. Maida. Every sentence has the respectful "*po*" at the end, used when speaking to older people in the Philippines. Or sometimes he would call me "*Ate* Maida", meaning older sister. While the reference to an older person initially bothered me, reminding me I was much older, his kind Filipino ways easily endeared me. It was soothing to speak in your native tongue every day. We would talk about little details of life. One day he greeted me with the sad news, "*Ate* Maida, *namatay na si Francis Magalona*" referring to the sudden death of the famous Filipino Master Rapper due to leukemia at the age of 46. When Manny Pacquiao, the first Filipino and only Asian boxer to win four world titles, won the Dream Match against Oscar de la Joya with a knock out on the eight round, Rom beamed with pride. He joyfully shared the news with me, spreading the glorious moment of a fellow countryman's victory. And one day, he asked if I knew any Filipino looking for a room, for he had a spare room he wanted to lease in his new home in Admiralty.

His Story

Rom is one of the estimated 150,000 Filipinos working in Singapore, accounting for about 3.2 percent of the 4.6 million population of Singapore.

Something inside me knew there was a story waiting to be told. I asked if I could interview him for this book. He initially hesitated, saying he really had no story to share. After some prodding, he finally agreed. We figured it would be best before his shift, which began at 4 pm and ended past midnight.

There is a staggering 11 million overseas Filipino workers, accounting for 11 percent of the total Filipino population. Called OFWs, they sent 15 billion dollars home last year to the Philippines, accounting for about 10 percent of the country's GDP. This 26-year-old barista is not only one, but is also the son of two overseas Filipino workers. His mother is a nurse who has been working in Saudi Arabia for almost three decades now, and his father was once selling copper tools also in Saudi Arabia. Rom was born there, as were his three younger sisters. The first three years of his life were spent there with his mom and dad.

At age three, he moved to the Philippines under the care of his grandmother in Bulacan, a province immediately north of Metro Manila. In a country where fair skin is highly valued, this cute and fair-skinned little boy instantly became the favorite grandchild of his maternal *lola* (grandmother). But after three years, his parents decided he was getting spoiled. They decided he should live with his paternal grandparents in Cavite instead, about 30 kilometers south of Manila. Very close to his maternal grandmother, the young boy was very much distraught by the separation. He could stay with his maternal grandmother on school holidays, but had to return to his paternal grandparents for school. It was a very painful parting for both grandmother and the young boy, causing them both much tears. Unlike his maternal grandmother's gentle ways, his father's parents were harsh. They punished the young boy when he did wrong, forcing him to kneel on the floor littered with rock salt.

His mom and dad would return for holidays in the Philippines for Christmas and summer, but that was only a few days in the year. When he was in his third year of high school, his parents finally decided to move back to the Philippines. Yet their son was no longer accustomed to having them around. He was not used to the strict and harsh ways of his father. Hence, their homecoming caused too much friction for their only son and his father. When he was blamed for accepting a bad bank cheque while tending to the family-run business, it was the last straw. He ran away from home. His father did not budge. He did not ask his only son to come back home, or make any contact with him.

Rom's beloved grandmother and maternal aunt helped him with his tuition fee in his last year of high school. Throughout university, his aunt paid for his tuition, and the young Rom worked part-time in Jollibee (the local version of McDonald's) for pocket money for his day-to-day expenses. At age 19, he started working for Starbucks, where he met and fell in love with a fellow barista, seven years his senior, who soon became his wife. By 22, the young Starbucks employee became a father.

When the young couple had a second child, the income of a Starbucks barista was no longer sufficient to pay for rent and their day-to-day needs. Their once blissful union was now characterized with many fights and arguments due to money issues. It was at this point that Rom decided to look for employment in either Canada or Singapore through an employment agency. While he found a job in Canada, it meant he could not come and see his family for two years. He figured Singapore would be better.

With tears rolling down his eyes, he tells me how painful it was to leave the Philippines. After working in Starbucks for six years, he was about to be promoted to be the store manager for the Starbucks branch inside the Asian Development Bank headquarters. He loved working in this company. "I was happy in Starbucks. I didn't want to leave," he tells me. It made him so upset that he and his wife had to fight just because of money. He told his wife, "I will leave the country for you. Even if it hurts me, I will do it for the benefit of our children."

Willing to sacrifice for his children, moving to another country was the only way he knew he could provide for his family. But the employment agency required a P150,000 (about 5,000 SGD) fee to secure him a job in Singapore. To pay the exorbitant placement fee, they used the ready credit in four credit cards: his, his wife, and even his wife's friend, and sister.

In February 2008, Rom moved to Singapore to work in a café called TCC (The Coffee Connoisseur). He stayed in a HDB flat in Ang Mo Kio, owned by a Filipina woman, Auntie Merlee, who was married to a Singaporean. In her four-bedroom HBD unit, one room was for the husband, wife and their teenaged son. They had a longtime tenant, a Malaysian, renting another room. The third room was rented out to four Filipino men working in TCC, and the last room was rented out to four women working in Burger King. Each paid $250 rent, allowing Auntie Merlee to easily earn $2000 from the two rooms.

This young father had always been free from vice: he did not smoke, drink or even spend a lot of time hanging out with male friends (*pagbabarkada*). He only had two close friends. Spending time at home with his family always came first. His weekend routine was to bring his kids to a play area called Fun Ranch, close to their home.

Hence, moving to Singapore without his family was tough. For the first month, Rom would cry every single day. Auntie Merlee's husband flew to Vietnam regularly for work, so Rom would ask him to buy him a bottle of Chivas Regal or Johnny Walker Black Label from the duty free store. He would drink so he could sleep. At first a bottle lasted two weeks. Then he could drink a bottle in one week. His body was soon looking for the alcohol when he woke up, numbing him from the pain of the separation from his family. His housemates started to notice that he was drinking a lot. After finishing four bottles, he stopped. It was not a cheap vice for it cost him $42 a bottle, which he had to subtract from his already limited living expenses.

The devoted husband and father scrimped every way he could so he could send home 78 percent of his salary to pay for the credit card debt and to provide for his family's needs. Very little was left for him to survive daily and pay his rent in Singapore. On Sundays, he would volunteer to cook for his roommates in exchange for a free meal. He would even offer to wash their laundry for a fee. Anything pretty much just to make ends meet. When the roommates had no money, they would sauté a can of *sotong* (squid) with garlic, onion, and tomatoes, and eat it with rice. Rom fondly remembers this humble meal, for it bonded him with his roommates.

Phone calls and sending text messages to his family soothed the loneliness and longing for home. But he too had to control his phone expenses, making his $20 phone card last at least for a week or at the most buy four calling cards within a month.

Working six days a week at TCC in the city's business district, he was fortunate to get Sundays off. He religiously went to church at Novena. Learning from his maternal grandmother, he prayed to God not for material blessings or money, which he desperately needed. Instead he prayed for strength and courage to get him through his ordeal. He did not explore Singapore's malls or tourist offerings, for he did not have the means to do that. Instead, he would head back home after going to church.

During the first six months he was away, his wife worked in Manila at a call center to augment the family income. She then followed her husband to Singapore, obtaining an EPEC pass to find a job. She was fortunate enough to find a job within a month with the transport company SBS. Living in a room in Yishun for three months, Rom and his wife missed their children immensely. They left their two youngsters in the care of a maid in Manila. Thanks to his mother's generosity in funding their airfare, his sister-in-law brought the two kids to Singapore on the 24th of December. This was the biggest Christmas gift Rom could ever ask for. He had not seen his children for almost a year.

Reunited with their children, five-year-old daughter Naomi and three-year-old son Nico, and their faithful maid, the young Filipino family started life anew in Singapore. They are now renting their own two-bedroom HDB unit in Admiralty. They have applied for Permanent Residency and are awaiting the results. In the meantime, their daughter Naomi, a very bright child, is raring to go to school. With Rom working on weekends in Starbucks, the family gets some time to go to church together on Sundays at St. Anthony in Woodlands. When Rom is off from work, he takes the kids to the playground near their home. On other times, they go to Sentosa or Causeway Point during the weekends. He has treated his family to a special holiday at the theme park in Genting island in Malaysia.

Rom has been working for five months now as Assistant Store Manager at the Raffles City Branch of Starbucks. He pushes himself to excel in his job, with the future of his kids in mind. He is accustomed to serving an expat clientele, as his stores in Manila had a good number of expatriates too. In the beginning, it was difficult to understand the way Singaporeans spoke. At work, his staff would either be Malay or Chinese, comprised of young baristas in their teens or early twenties. Not understanding their language, he would sometimes jokingly say, "Are you talking about me?" or "We should all be like Channel 5, speak in English please." He has been commended for having good partner connection. Using the Filipino value of *pakikisama*, he cleverly finds ways to foster harmonious relations with all the members of his team.

With much discipline, he does not go out and spend on unnecessary things. His wife has some Filipino friends, former colleagues in the call center and bank in Manila who have now moved to Singapore. Allan, Rom's colleague in the Starbucks in Manila, is his dearest friend.

As the tears well in his eyes, he confides that his family means the world to him, and he would do anything to provide the best for them. Having grown up with absentee parents, and both Rom and his wife have divorced parents, he does not want his children to experience what he had experienced. He wants to give them financial stability and for them to grow up in a safe place. This is what Singapore is offering him.

When he meets Filipinos who have just moved here, or other new migrants, he advises them: "When you get a job, you must love your job. Don't complain. Make the best of it, for many remain without jobs for many months." He recognizes that the precious opportunity he has now is something he will not attain in the Philippines.

The family is still living on a tight budget. There is still a big credit card debt to be paid. Every bit of spending is recorded in the ledger his wife keeps at home, monitoring every single expense. Yet, he is already very grateful that he is happily living a simple, comfortable life with his family.

Noticing the time on his watch, he takes a last sip of Coke, then respectfully ask to be excused so he can make it to Starbucks on time for his shift. His workday ends past 1 am in the morning, after the store has been closed, cleaned, and prepared for the next day.

This young father has left me all choked up. Working as a writer in Singapore where the cost of living is high, I myself am in a financially challenging state. But as a single woman, my situation is entirely different. I only have my needs to tend to. Long after Rom has left, I remain affected by his story and the rawness of his emotions. I admire his selflessness, and his determination in providing well for his family.

It reminds me of how my own father sacrificed much, as he was committed to providing the best education he could afford to give me. When I was admitted into one of the best colleges in the US, he generously worked long hours to make the dream happen. The experience of being away from your family was familiar to me. But Rom's experience of separation from his children and of living with so little, I could only imagine. Many Filipinos experience this in Singapore. Many other foreign workers go through what Rom had gone through, some living in much harsher conditions.

While my life in Singapore has much room for improvement, I feel blessed with the comfortable living and work conditions I have. It also becomes clear to me that I have the responsibility to seize the daily opportunities and to make the most of my life. It is not just for myself, but also for my parents who have lovingly provided the best for me.

19

Single White Female in Little India

Alexandra Schmutterer, German
37 years old, Marketing Professional,
Moved to Singapore in May 2006, Single

How We Met

With the duties on liquor in Singapore, alcoholic beverage are not cheap. But trust the ingenuity of expats to find clever ways to get a free drink in this island. One Australian artist told me she goes to art exhibit openings for her free booze. There too are openings of bars and restaurants which offer special invites. My job as a food and travel writer requires me to check out these new places and I recently received an invite for one of these bar openings. It was for the opening of Aqua, and the invite even had a special password guests have to utter to enter the party. It was at Robertson Quay, and a long queue had already formed outside by the time I got there. The crowd was dominantly expat and the place was packed, with the offer of free champagne and beer at the bar.

The bartender was in high spirits as a crowd gathered to collect their glasses of booze. He teased, "Doesn't anyone want coffee or water?" And with only two bartenders attending to the crowd, it was a long wait. A guy caught my eye and offered to get me a drink. But in the end, the bartender ended up handing me a glass of champagne first. I walked away from the bar, but didn't get far when the same guy walked my way. My friend and usual accomplice to such events had to beg off at the last minute, unable to get off work early, so I was alone. The guy was waiting for a friend. And so we ended up chatting away. He was German and had just moved to Singapore a few months before. The conversation was easy. After chatting for a long time, his friend arrived. She was a beautiful, tall German lady. At that point, I took it as my cue to head off for I thought I might be rudely interrupting their date.

The guy offered to head back to the bar to get another glass of champagne for me, but apparently there was no more wine or beer being served. Alex, the tall German lady, and I started to chat. With no free booze and our tummies grumbling, all three of us agreed to grab a bite. We ended up at Jumbo, with Sven, the German guy, making the order in fluent Mandarin. Each time a dish arrived, the Chinese woman would look at me and address me in Mandarin, only to have Sven answer back in Mandarin. It totally threw her off. Alex and I found ourselves laughing at how hilarious the situation was. Truly, I looked Asian, with many thinking I am Chinese.

A young waitress who didn't speak English, and obviously a recent arrival from China, Tsing Tsao (where the famous beer is made) to be exact, was serving us. She was obviously thrilled to meet our German Chinese-speaking companion. As Alex pointed out, "It doesn't get better than this for her—he's *ang moh* and she doesn't even have to speak English. He speaks Mandarin."

We all exchanged contact details that evening, but it took several months before Alex and I caught up with each other. We finally arranged to meet for lunch on Valentine's Day.

I had taken the bus to get to Dempsey and for the first time I was stuck in bumper to bumper traffic in Singapore. There was a construction along Farrer Road, causing the cars to be at a standstill. I ended up getting off the bus, walking until two bus stops away, and then took a cab to Dempsey. I explained to Alex what happened. She totally understood for she too took the bus or MRT to get around Singapore. Then we realized, both being on non-expat salaries, we had much in common. Our lunch in PS Café in Dempsey turned into a chat fest lasting for almost four hours. Talking about anything and everything, we immediately transitioned from being mere acquaintances into friends.

Her Story

Taking up Alex's offer to see her new place in Little India, I took the bus to her apartment, conveniently located just outside the Farrer MRT Station.

I buzzed on the intercom, and she let me inside her building. When she opened the door, I was surprised to see a gorgeous two-level apartment with a spacious patio, ideal for entertaining. The dining table was set with plates, cutlery, wine glasses, and candles, as if a romantic dinner was in the works. On the first level was a full bathroom, two towering shelves of books, her dining table, and an empty area awaiting a sofa. She led me up the second floor, with a blank white slate on the stairway, perfect for displaying art work. She had cleverly installed a closet outside her room. Her bedroom had a commanding queen size bed with an elegant hardwood bed frame, and it had its own bathroom and a glass door opening onto the patio looking out to Little India. She told me it is peaceful on a Saturday night, but very noisy on Sundays when a plethora of Bangladeshi workers gather here on their day off. But we both agreed it is a small price to pay for such a beautiful apartment, centrally located in the city and at an affordable price.

Thirty-seven-year-old Alex works at Siemens as a PR Manager. Her colleagues are shocked when she tells them she lives in Little India. It is not usual for an *ang moh*, more so a Single White Female, to choose to live in Little India. But Alex loves it. Without a car or an expat package, she is careful with her expenses. This apartment is conveniently located two stops away from her place of work and the rent is suited to her budget. Having Mustafa, a giant department store and supermarket selling everything from appliances to specialty food, close by and open 24 hours is an added bonus. Farrer Market with numerous hawker stalls is an added attraction too.

Alex moved to Singapore in May 2006 from her hometown in Munich, Germany. Living in Germany all her life, she was ready to live somewhere else in the world. It was a move orchestrated with her then boyfriend. It was a toss-up between Singapore and Hong Kong. Her boyfriend grew up in Hong Kong, and Alex would much rather have a fresh start in a new city. They had a difficult time finding a place to rent, even with the help of the real estate agent provided by her boyfriend's company. After three weeks, Alex took matters into her hands and found a place at Robertson Quay. The relationship did not work out, yet she continued sharing the condominium with her ex-boyfriend. It was almost a year after the break up that she finally found her own place in Little India. She did not enlist the help of an agent. She merely relied on discipline and persistence in calling and checking out rentals in Chinatown and Little India.

One of her pet peeves about rentals in Singapore is that they do not come with a dishwasher. She pestered her previous agent about where to find a tabletop dishwasher. After some research, she found the German company Bosch to produce a compact little dishwasher she has installed in her compact kitchen. Only slightly bigger than a microwave oven, her guests are often baffled what it is. She told me, "We Germans are lazy. We can't be bothered washing dishes, so I really need this." Her other luxury is having a cleaning lady come every week. In Munich, she had a cleaning lady for she did not want to spend her weekends cleaning. Here in Singapore, she hires an absent-minded Filipino domestic helper called Marilyn, who comes once a week.

Over a bottle of wine and home-cooked spaghetti bolognese, Alex and I talked about life in Singapore. At her workplace, her colleagues often head out for lunch without inviting her. The Singaporean Chinese head off together, and the Indians head off together. She is then left with the option of either eating alone or seeking other expats who wish to have lunch with her. Working on weekends is also unheard off in Germany. She tells me that in fact you have to get permission to work on weekends. Here it is nothing unusual.

She enjoys the weather in Singapore but is baffled by many things in this island. Frequently getting around by bus, she has noticed how older Singaporeans would tap the seat in the bus before sitting down. She then asked her colleagues what that was all about, and they told her it was so they don't get hemorrhoids. I've never heard of people tapping chairs in the bus before, but I also wondered if this illness is contagious that way.

When I first met Alex and Sven, they told me how shocking it was for them to meet people who view shopping and watching TV as their hobbies. No one in Germany would ever say that. For Alex, shopping means heading to the store to buy something you need. In her case, it is often things from Ikea that she needs for her apartment. But for many people in Singapore, shopping can entail hours of window-shopping and not actually buying anything. She has not shopped for clothes or shoes, as they do not fit well on her tall frame, plus they are often more expensive. Perhaps many Singaporeans would be shocked to find out that she does not have a single television set in her home. Alex tells me, "Why would I need a TV set, when I have friends?" After work, she always finds people to meet or things to do. She too is a voracious reader, happily left alone in the company of a good book.

Just like the majority of Singapore's population who partake of meals from the hawker center, Alex feels right at home doing this. Unlike many expats who are peeved by the Singaporean practice of using a packet of tissue to "chope" (reserve) a table at hawker centers, this German woman is unfazed by it. She tells me that Germans are known in Europe to do the same. "Go to a resort in Spain and you will find them waking up early to save a sunbed by the pool or by the beach. Then they will go back to sleep, only to get up right before lunch to enjoy their reserved seat."

Holidays require a bit of getting used to for Alex. Christmas is huge in Germany, where the snow and family dinners create the winter festive celebrations. She finds it awfully quiet here. But one holiday she has quite a bit of experience in is Chinese New Year. In their office, the ritual of *lo-hei*, the traditional tossing of *yu sheng* (a raw fish salad with shredded vegetables), is practiced during a long lunch or dinner banquet with colleagues. All the diners gather at the table to toss the salad to ensure a prosperous business year. *Yu sheng* implies an abundance of wealth and long life and is a must at every New Year's celebration. In addition to the *yu sheng* salad, a spread of sharks' fin, abalone, sea cucumber, fish, chicken and vegetable dishes are served. The meal lasts for about three hours. Alex does not eat shark's fin. After three hours of festivities with only the chicken and a few pieces of broccoli in her stomach, she leaves still hungry and goes to the nearest 7-11 and grabs an ice cream to fill her up.

Her advice to someone moving to Singapore, "Negotiate a good contract, including your housing and transport. Also, leave your winter clothes at home and bring your own furniture." She brought all her things along, with her winter clothes now stored under her stairway. Thinking the tropical climate would be ideal for cycling, she brought her bicycle as well, but she has only used it once. There are no bike paths in the city, and without a car, it is impossible to get to the east coast or Pulau Ubin to cycle there.

Having a great time, our conversation extended till the wee hours of the morning. With the MRT no longer running at this late hour, I took a cab home. The taxi driver was chatty but very respectful and by the end of my ride, I accidentally discovered how to deal with the 101 questions of drivers. I asked the driver about the 24-hour places to eat. The conversation flowed so easily and there were no questions about being single or stereotypes about your country of origin coming into play. The tables were now turned. Being a seasoned journalist, I interviewed him. When I learned he was from

Hainan, I asked the friendly uncle, "So how do you cook Hainanese chicken rice?" He got so animated in detailing the process that he was upset when we reached my condominium complex and he did not have enough time to discuss his recipe.

Hitting it off well, Alex and I naturally found many other occasions to catch up and continue our marathon conversations. She invited me for the opening of an exhibition featuring the work of Ketna Patel, where Kumar, a famous Singaporean-Indian drag queen entertainer, was the guest of honor. It was located at Boat Quay. She was running late, coming from her office in MacPherson Road.

Alex told me previously that one of her dates once took her to Boat Quay on a Friday night. While she did not hit it off with her date, she did notice that all around them were good-looking guys, kicking off the weekend with a couple of drinks. She said we should hit the scene one Friday night, just to have our fill of "eye candy". While waiting for her, I checked out the scene. And indeed, there were numerous "suits" hanging out. A suit I was dating told me they did more drinking now. Their jobs were in jeopardy because of the financial crisis, so pubs and bars were enjoying brisk business as they drank their anxieties and worries away.

The exhibition at the second floor of TCC was packed. The art by Ketna Patel called con-fusion featured Asia pop art and furniture, and the pieces were bright, bold, and too busy for my eyes. It was interesting, but seemed more suitable for an ad agency than a home. We looked at the art, while catching up on each other's lives. Wine flowed freely and we enjoyed an array of delectable finger food from The Coffee Conneisseur's menu. We cooled down with glasses of white wine and an extremely attentive waiter kept our glasses filled throughout the evening. Kumar got the room roaring in laughter. It was an expat crowd and he told them. "Hey, don't be too obvious that you're just here for the free booze and food." He also got me laughing when he said, "When people see in yoga class and they don't understand the teacher, they look at me. What do they think, I provide subtitles just because I'm Indian?" Alex and I thoroughly enjoyed the stand-up comic. We agreed to watch his show in the Esplanade a few weeks later.

When we met up, we were shocked that the entire Esplanade was filled to the brim. His sold-out performance meant that over a thousand people bought tickets to his show. His humor this time was geared to locals. In front of me was a Chinese guy in his thirties, rolling off his chair in laughter. He would make not so subtle jokes about top government officials. How bold and how unusual, yet I was impressed how he had a voice uniquely his own, respected in what was often called a repressed society.

Keeping to our promise, Alex and I met up one Friday night at Boat Quay for our fill of wine, beer, and eye-candy. Truly, there were some charming men. But none we met. We were again busy catching up on each other's lives. I was fighting a bad cough and felt somewhat feverish. Alex on the other hand had a bandaged foot, for a guy she was dating managed to somehow accidentally injure her foot. But still the conversation flowed. She told me a friend's friend on a business trip in Singapore would join us for a drink. When he arrived, he turned out to be an Egyptian living in Germany. My cough got the worst of me and his personality didn't quite appeal to me, so I headed home early for much-needed rest.

Like Alex, I would be the last person to say shopping is my hobby. I do not enjoy mindlessly wandering in crowded malls for an outfit. But with an upcoming trip to the US in a city promising highs of 40°F and my winter clothes stored in my family home in the Philippines, I had to find suitable clothing in Singapore. I was going to be in a conference to meet important people in my line of work and I definitely wanted to make a good impression. So I had to go shopping. After checking a few shops, I was not too keen to spend a lot of money for clothes I would use just for a few days. When Alex found out about my predicament, she insisted that I just borrow her winter clothes. She was tall and skinny like a model. Would it fit? She suggested I come over her house to choose a few pieces.

Emmanuel came along with me to Alex's home. All three of us immediately got into a long spirited conversation. We walked to Tekka for some chicken *murtabak* for dinner and washed it down with Tiger Beer. Dessert was chocolate *roti* for Alex and chocolate banana for me. The food stalls were closing by 10 pm. We bought a couple more bottles of Tiger to take back to her flat. After several hours of talking, Emmanuel asked Alex, "Wait…do you take bus 64 every morning?" She said, "Yes!" "Oh my gosh, you are the wet hair girl!?" Then he recounted how he would take the bus from his house in River Valley Road to his office in Dhoby Ghaut everyday. He would see Nick, a guy who would get on at the same bus stop. When the bus stopped at Robertson Quay, a girl with wet hair would get on, find the first seat available then proceed to read her book. Every single day this would happen. We were all amazed at how structured our lives had become. Like clockwork, the bus would arrive and the same people would get on. And this was made even more predictable by Singapore's efficiency, where the bus would arrive promptly every single day. I called it "familiar strangers". In a city of four million people going to the same places, there were familiar strangers. How odd that two of my friends had been crossing paths and never bothered to get to know each other. I made friends at the drop of a hat and freely talked to strangers, but Emmanuel was the exact opposite. If I did not talk to that guy at the bar and this tall German girl, I wouldn't have made such a good friend. "See, if you were friendlier, you would have gotten to know the wet hair girl."

Till about two in the morning, we drank Tiger Beer and talked about our woes and joys of living in Singapore. For about $10 each, we had a dinner, dessert and a couple of bottles of beers. Emmanuel and I bid Alex goodbye, holding bags filled with thick coats and a couple of sweaters she lent me. As she closed her front door and we got into the lift, I told Emmanuel, "I can't believe you knew the wet hair girl." He said, "I didn't expect her to be friendly at all. She looked so serious."

No matter where you come from or where you have been, living in Singapore will thrust you into the company of familiar strangers. The choice is yours. Do you open your lives to them or do you merely remain familiar strangers crossing paths often?

20

Livin' La Dolce Vita

Giovanni Lombardo, Italian
41 years old, Married with three kids,
Moved to Singapore in 2002

How We Met

Exhibit openings are plentiful in Singapore. When my friend Shawn asked if I was interested to join him at Discovery and Journey, an art exhibit opening at Hermes, I gladly said yes. It was one of those wet and yucky Singapore days. Shawn and I met at the entrance of Hermes along Liat Towers on Orchard Road. When he saw me smartly dressed for the occasion, this graphic designer then said, "Oh, I forgot to wear something nice." But despite the humble jeans and shirt number, artists like Shawn can get away with showing up in fancy events by simply appearing in their own eclectic fashion. It was Shawn's friend, Sherman, who had sent Shawn the invite. Sherman is a film director, and Shawn had acted for his documentary in the Singapore Biennale. Out of champagne, we settled for a fruit juice then headed to the second level. There, I met Giovanni and Adeline. Giovanni is an Italian, who immediately put me at ease uttering a few words in Tagalog. His companion Adeline is a Malaysian photographer. Both acted in Sherman's documentary, along with Shawn.

In minutes, Giovanni and I were talking about my 102-year-old grandmother and all sorts of things about the Philippines. The ease in our conversation made Sherman wonder if we had been friends for a long time. The exhibit on the third floor featured illustrations by Argentina-born artist Flavia Da Rin. The gallery recreated a fairy tale forest setting to complement the artwork filled with the fantasy of fairies, nymphs, and animals with butterfly wings. The artist welcomed guests, many of whom were *tai tais* of different nationalities. All were elegantly dressed, with perfectly manicured nails. Every strand of hair was perfectly in place. And almost everyone had their very own Birkin bag by Hermes dangling on their arm. The art was charming, with the innocence of a child, and an interesting touch where the artist used herself as the main character in work. Seeing her there was almost like playing spot the difference between her and her cartoon digital images. While the art was pleasant, it was the guests that intrigued me more.

Clustered together with Shawn and Sherman, we quietly people watched. And in hushed murmurs, I asked them, "Do you think coming here is the only thing they had to do today?" The women looked so polished and perfect. They epitomized the stereotypical image of *tai tais*, women of leisure in Singapore who are said to play tennis in the air-conditioned courts of the Four Seasons, spend hours over coffee and tea with their friends, and shop in the chic boutiques along Orchard. There is no need to look after the kids for they easily have a maid or two to do so.

After getting our dose of the art and the company of women with powdered noses, Sherman, Shawn and I returned down to the second floor to join Giovanni and Adeline. Amidst the expensive boutique items, we laughed and chatted while sipping the now replenished supply of champagne.

Giovanni and I exchanged numbers and stayed in touch. The next Sunday, Giovanni invited me to join him and a gorgeous single Italian to KM8 at Sentosa. My conservative upbringing made me wonder if it was appropriate to encourage a friendship with this Italian married man. But with another single guy for company, it should be fine. Giovanni picked me up at Newton MRT, but to my surprise there was no single hot Italian man with him. Instead, it was Adeline sitting shotgun. My Italian friend explained that his guest chose to go shopping instead of watching the sunset at Sentosa.

I asked Giovanni if there was a big party going on at KM8. He shook his head. I later learned that watching the sunset on a Sunday evening is a weekly treat he indulges in. Basking in the sun makes him grateful for the week that has passed and gives him energy for the busy week ahead. Sitting on beach towels, we comfortably gaze towards the sun. Then as the sun slowly made its gentle descent, the stories came pouring out. I probed what brought them here. Adeline grew up in Malaysia, studied at a university in the US, and eventually moved to work in Singapore. Giovanni's story on the other hand was a riveting adventure involving a severe motorcycle accident in Cyprus in his early 20s.

His Story

Wanting to hear more of Giovanni's story, I asked to interview him. We agreed on a cheap and cheerful dinner at his favorite stall at the East Coast Laguna. However, he had some wine deliveries scheduled at Holland Village first and his meeting with his clients extended beyond the scheduled time. The gentleman that he is, Giovanni offered to treat me for lunch the next day at Garibaldi, one of the best Italian restaurants in Singapore.

As I walk along Purvis street and its traditional shophouses, I spot Giovanni just outside the restaurant chatting with a mate. After the warm greeting and pecks on both sides of the cheek, his male companion is impressed. Giovanni introduces me to him. And the guy, who turns out to be German, says, "Wow, life isn't fair. You get to have lunch with this beautiful lady. And I get to have lunch with him (referring to another German guy smoking a cigar close by)." Giovanni converses with him in fluent German. To the guy smoking the cigar, he speaks Finnish. He gives them flyers of the Italian wines he is selling, with his contact details and prices. And ever so smoothly, he ask for their business cards. Both gentlemen happily grant his request. The two men walk into the restaurant, and we follow just behind them. I then learn that this enterprising wine merchant cleverly networked while he was waiting a few minutes outside the restaurant for my arrival. And these two gentlemen he exchanged a few words with have instantly become potential customers for his wine business.

As we sit at our table, I tell Giovanni that he obviously looks happy. He says, "How can I not be happy, I am with you. And you are as beautiful as I remember you to be the first time we met." Unsure how to react to the flirtation and flattery, I laugh, "You surely are an Italian."

I still cannot shake off the quick connection he made outside. He truly made an impression with the two gentlemen, easily putting them at ease. More so, I am surprised to learn the fact that he speaks eight languages, which impresses not just me but his two prospective buyers. I then probe my lunch companion, "So what are the eight languages you speak?" He lists them all, "English, Italian, German, French, Greek, Spanish, Portuguese, and Bahasa."

We settle into our meal, with Giovanni thoughtfully asking how I am and how my life is going. I explain that I am making a go of my life as a writer here in Singapore in a not so typical way. He then tells me, "You know Maida, everyday I am awake at 6 am, I drive my kids and wife to school. She is a schoolteacher. I buy a croissant from Délifrance and go home to eat it while having my cup of coffee and reading the papers. My neighbors in my HDB block ask me why I am not working. I tell them jokingly that I was retrenched." Seeing him at home during the day, his neighbors think he is unemployed. They do not comprehend the unusual nature of his work. "They don't understand that when I am at home on the computer translating documents I am working, or when I am corresponding through email with my clients I am working, or when I go to restaurants like this and network like I did outside or with the restaurant manager, I am working."

Giovanni imports fine Italian wines and has a steady stream of translating jobs, which require him to translate documents from English to Greek, Italian, or any of the eight languages he knows. I am intrigued how he has learned them all. "If I tell you, you will not believe me, you will think I am an Italian joker," the natural linguist tells me.

"Sure, surprise me!" I gamely retort. He begins to explain:

"When you are a young boy growing up in Venice, there are cruise people from all over the world. You are not surprised to see a black man, an Indian or a Chinese. When you are grown up, say you are 15, and live on an Italian beach like Lido, people there are so liberal. The Scandinavian women are topless or in a G-string. Of course Italian girls your age are very conservative because they are still living with their parents. The girls who are from Austria and Scandinavia, when they go to the beach they just want to enjoy the beach and the sunshine. They are not staying with mommy. These people speak different languages so when you want to make good with foreign women, you try to learn the language. From age 16 to 26, it was a learning process for me."

He taught himself with the help of books, magazines, newspapers, and movies.

I am amazed at how a young Italian boy cleverly learned languages for the purpose of flirting with women. But to Giovanni this is almost common sense. "I talk to people because language is not an academic subject. It's a tool to interact with people. We don't need to go to school for that."

There was an engineer who managed a business buying water purification and sanitation equipment from Germany, but he did not speak the language. He asked Giovanni to go along with him and translate. Giovanni was 24 at that time. The young Italian grabbed the opportunity for easy money. Then he took a holiday alone in Cyprus. But as fate would have it, a truck collided with him as he was riding a Vespa. The accident left him comatose for six days. His parents were on holiday then and there were no email or mobile phones then to locate them. He had a choice to feel sorry for himself or to get better. He chose the latter. He still has scars from the accident to show to this day, but the determined Italian recovered fully.

Since Giovanni had no liability for the accident, he received monetary compensation for his injury. While he was recovering, his mother died after a long battle with cancer and his father became very lonely and sad. "It was very difficult to go through these things. So I told my best friend Marco that since we were young and had no obligations, we should go and see the world. We didn't know where to go, so we went to Sri Lanka."

He didn't know much about Sri Lanka except for what he read in a book. "I was very fascinated by the country because 1,500 years ago, there was a king who made a huge basin to collect the rain water. Sri Lanka would be very much dryer than how it is now if this genius of a king did not built all these basins. One is called Samudra, like a lake. I was amazed by the historical things." His trip to Sri Lanka was his first encounter of life outside Europe. It was a startling awakening he describes: "I was also saddened by my meeting with a non-European society. It was a society founded in inequality, on exploitation and the things we got rid of in the French revolution." The trip succeeded in distracting him from his mother's death and his accident, but the immersion into Sri Lanka's poverty and diseases were just too much for Giovanni. He was ready to continue his journey to another place, "Sri Lanka is beautiful. But I wanted to go to a place where people seem to be well off and middle class, and a society different from what I know."

He told Marco he wanted to go to Hong Kong. His best buddy thought he was crazy. So they reached a compromise. Marco said, "You go to Hong Kong. You use Singapore Airlines, stopover at Singapore and then we'll go to Malaysia for three or four days, then to Tioman Island, then we go to your Hongkong, then back to Singapore, then Colombo, then back to Italy." I said "Deal!" We did this and then I met this Singaporean woman with her friend in Pulau Tioman. She was on a holiday with her good friend."

Giovanni was pleased with the trip to Singapore in 1994. He recalls, "I was pleasantly surprised with the safety, the food, and that there were no starving people or leprosy victims without limbs on the streets (as he had seen in Sri Lanka)." Little did he know that the Singaporean woman he met in Tioman would eventually become his wife. He also did not predict he would eventually be living in Singapore.

Giovanni has been married for 11 years now. They lived in Italy for three years but his wife had a hard time there, being a non-European foreigner. It was putting a strain on their marriage. So his wife suggested that if she could find him a job in Singapore, they would move back together. She successfully found him a job as a Marketing Manager for a restaurant company.

The trooper that he is, Giovanni moved to Singapore, along with his wife and their son and daughter. They have been living in a HDB unit in the heartland of Yishun so his wife can live close to her parents. The unassuming person that he is, Giovanni can't understand why Europeans have to live in a condominium when they move to Singapore when they lived in narrow dwellings too in Europe. Filled with contentment, he tells me, "Life is simple here. There are no seasons, so there is no need to buy lots of clothes." The added perk he says, "I can go to be the beach every week."

Once he started to conduct business with the Singaporeans, he soon realized that this society has conflicting values from his own culture. He tells me, "The things not valued in my country are valued here. The things that are not important in my country are important here."

The Italians warmly greet anyone they encounter. In contrast he tells me, "Here they just grunt. They just speak by grunts."

Italians savor the sweetness of life, *La Dolce Vita*. In contrast, here in Singapore he says, "Everything must be related to money, which is sad. Never in my life would I see a friend for work. In Italy, work is work. Business is business. Life is life. I go out to enjoy myself."

Giovanni has learnt that running a business here is totally different from what he was accustomed to. He narrates:

"I did not know the Asian way of face saving. I was in the losing end of many transactions. In Italy, if you are wrong you are wrong. And also if you are wrong, you are ashamed to be wrong, so you try not to be wrong or to do anything wrong. Here, the important thing is not to be rude, so if someone did not pay for your invoice for instance, or if someone asked for a discount which is beyond the reasonable price, you don't have to be angry, you just smile and say it's not possible. If you become angry or irritated or rude, the focus is no longer I am right and you are wrong. The focus of the issue is you are rude, which is much more important than the previous issue for which we will never focus on anymore. And to me this was a shock."

Even the systems at work baffled him. Giovanni compares it to his past experience, "Before, I was an export manager in a company that made fashion accessories. So I was traveling all around the world with the company's credit card. My boss trusted me. When I came here, I saw some amazing practices. If the printer ran out of ink, I had to buy the ink first and show the bill to the accounts department, and then I will get my petty cash voucher. It is something completely not understandable to me."

In 2005, his expat friends suggested he start his own business importing Italian products, mostly wines. His business is now successfully supplying Italian restaurants and some corporate functions.

He revels in thinking out of the box and tells me how naturally it comes for him. "I came across a function of a big Japanese company. I wanted to get all their name cards. So I thought I would invest in one bottle of wine. I approached them announcing, 'Hello, I have a surprise for you. I will have a lucky draw. Please put your name card into a bucket.' A very beautiful lady walked in and I asked her to pick the winner." At the end of the night, someone happily won a fine bottle of Italian wine, and Giovanni had access to all these new contacts. He points out, "Something like this they don't teach you in a book. You have to have an attitude towards it."

It is this positive attitude towards life that Giovanni enjoys everyday. He finds delight in connecting with people, be it through language, wine or food. "Wine is a very interesting thing, it brings people together." With his varied interests, Giovanni easily makes friends in Singapore. "I meet my friends through like-minded interests. I met some friends through my work in advertising, commercials, and movies, and I met others through wine sales, art exhibitions, ceramic workshops at the community art center, openings and others." He states the obvious, "I love to network with people from everywhere." Speaking eight languages helps too, "I don't feel limited to talking to Italians or English-speaking people."

Food is also his means to connect with others. The passionate Italian who can cook Sri Lankan curries, Jamaican dishes, and his beloved Italian pastas says passionately, "Like language, food is also an important tool in understanding people. People here say, "Have you eaten?"—that means how are you." In his culture, dining is an art form. It is never rushed. He is grateful that he can choose whom he dines with, for he never eats with someone who rushes through a meal.

It seems like this is home for his family. His children are well adjusted in the public school. "To my knowledge, my ten-year-old son has five girls who like him very much. My daughter is Malay-Italian and she has many friends. She doesn't have any biases against the Indians or the Chinese.

His weekends are devoted to his children. "I like to talk to them, to interact with them. They are very intelligent and ask me many questions. I don't like to tell them, don't do this or don't do that…" He is amazed at how they learn concepts on their own. "In Europe, we had the French Revolution, Scientific Revolution and had the enlightenment. Here, they have ghost, spirits, beliefs, and other superstitions. We don't believe in ghosts anymore. I just laugh at it. My children too are not afraid. They laugh at it. And interestingly, I did not teach them that."

Giovanni tells me that when his youngest child was born in Singapore, other people were concerned about the confinement period, the practice of staying indoors for the baby and mother for the first month after the birth. Under the care of a confinement nanny, there are certain superstitions and rituals to follow. The practical Italian tells me, "We don't have it in Italy. After the first week, I took the baby to the beach with me. I never followed the confinement rules. The baby just needs to eat and sleep. You just have to clean their shit. They can't do that for themselves."

After two hours, we finish savoring our leisurely lunch. I thank him for the wonderful meal. As we prepare to part, I tell him I am walking to Raffles City and he offers to walk with me to the bank. As we walk on North Bridge Road, he smiles as he basks in the warm sunshine, "I'm glad I walked with you. I wouldn't have thought of walking here. Next time, I will." It is this openness to all things and the appreciation of the little details that makes life sweeter for this Italian. Just like a true Italian, he lives *la dolce vita*. I guess you can take the Italian out of Italy, but deep in his heart the passion and love for the sweet life always remains. Even in Singapore.

21

Every Breath You Take

Kiran Singh, Indian,
48 years old, Meditation Teacher,
Moved to Singapore in 2001, Married with two children

How We Met

My journey to Singapore was a short three and a half-hour trip from my home in Manila. I was fortunate that I easily found a wonderful home in three days with an amazing woman to share it with. But one thing I learned through the years is that the journey never ends when you land in one place. Our life is in itself the journey. And the work of constantly finding internal peace and happiness wherever you are or whoever you are with is both a challenge and personal responsibility.

Prior to moving to Singapore, many people commented how they were sure I would get bored here. They were certain it is such a young country and that there is nothing to do here. Yes, it is a young society. I was shocked to discover my 102-year-old grandmother's photos were much older than a historical photography exhibit at the National Museum. When I researched about attractions in Singapore, I realized that the Bedok Reservoir is as old as my best friend's career in advertising.

So far, I have managed to happily amuse myself and find things to do in this island. But as I search for the soul of this nation, I am bothered. The aspirations of many Singaporeans are summarized in the four Cs: Country Club, Credit card, Car, and Condominium. This is confirmed by the long queues to get into the Louis Vuitton store in Takashimaya. The many Jaguars on the road also attest to how rich this country is.

But for someone not interested in the four Cs, an emptiness pervades. And one path I have taken in Singapore is a path to stillness and meditation. I have been practicing zen meditation for three years now. I meditate every morning after going for my daily walk. Sometimes it is easy to get into the meditation, but other times I find myself easily distracted. Wanting to deepen my practice and to find a sangha to sit with, I found a Buddhist meditation class offered at Neil Road in Chinatown for three consecutive Fridays. With my flatmate as my companion, we sat as a nun with short-cropped hair and a saffron and golden yellow robe guided us through the basics of meditation. It was from 7:30 to 9 pm on a Friday night, what my friends described as primetime drinking time. While we took care of our spirit, many others were drowning their sorrows in spirits. We paid full attention to our breathing and meditation in the heart of Chinatown, while outside there was a lion dance, with the beat of the drums challenging our meditation practice.

I continued practicing meditation on my own, but still struggled each day. I dated a guy who practiced meditation for 30 minutes every day and he suggested I take the Art of Living workshop.

With much respect for this guy, I took his word and looked up the Art of Living website. Unprepared to take a full course and coughing up several hundred dollars, I took the free meditation and yoga workshop instead one Saturday afternoon. I headed to the Art of Living studio at North Bridge Road, across the national library. I was almost late for the class and had to run from Bugis MRT in order to make it there in time. There was my teacher Kiran, dressed in Indian Kurta.

I am one person who is clearly drawn to people's energies. And Kiran's energy was clearly positive. I arrived frazzled and sweaty, only to find one other participant sitting on the yoga mat, a lady banker dressed for the gym. Later, four Indian participants joined us, including a husband and wife who insisted their two-year-old daughter would happily sit still as they meditated. Dressed in her party dress and an ankle bracelet that jingled, I saw the little toddler as distracting. So did Kiran, who gently asked the insistent parents to please take the child down while we exhaled the toxins from our body.

As she jogged in place in her Indian outfit, she put all her energy into the exercise. Not conscious if she looked silly, she beamed a great big smile. She talked to each one of us on why we joined this class, and she was soon calling me dear. It was that motherly warmth that she had. She taught us some yoga and breathing meditation techniques. At the end of the class, I felt relaxed and ready to face the rest of the day. I noticed myself to be more mindful, more energized, and more alert in my interactions with people for the rest of the day.

Her Story

Attracted by Kiran's gentle ways, I ask to meet up for coffee. She kindly accommodates, choosing to meet in a café in Harborfront, close to her husand's workplace. She arrives with her 23-year-old daughter Simran. She apologizes for arriving late, as she has come from the weekly meditation session held in her home in Clementi.

This 47-year-old mother radiates a certain peace and calm when she smiles. While I wait for my tea, I overhear her sweetly relating to her daughter. "How was your sleep?" and her daughter lovingly responds to her mom. It is a vision to see such a harmonious relationship between mother and child. Kiran is dressed in a cool white linen blouse, while her daughter is clad in a purple blouse with gold accessories and earrings.

Kiran was born in Northern India. In 1983, she married a sailor. This began an adventure as she accompanied her husband and traveled the seas to many different parts of the world. With their two children, they settled in Bombay in 1991 for nine years, followed by two years in Hong Kong, until they finally moved for an onshore posting in Singapore in 2001.

Kiran describes her shift to the Lion City, "The culture in Hong Kong is different as compared to Singapore. They are not as open to expats as the people in Singapore are. English is not as well spoken among the Chinese community." Accustomed to moving around, Kiran observes this transition was easier than their previous moves: "Moving from Bombay to Hong Kong was not easy for us. We lived there for nine years and had our own comfort zone, our own way of life, and then we had to move to a new country. Then suddenly after two years, we found out that we had to move to Singapore. Initially, I was not sure how things would be like. Singapore being close to the equator, I had to be mentally prepared that Singapore is going to be hot, hotter, and hottest."

But her initial impressions were very positive. She recalls, "The moment we landed in Singapore, I noticed so much greenery and how clean it was. I really felt good, that was my first reaction." Settling in was quite easy, with the exception of getting adjusted to eating their meals out. But in Singapore, it is the norm to buy food from the hawker centers. In fact, it is cheaper to do so than to cook a meal at home. She narrates her initial immersion to the food culture here: "At first, there were no cooking facilities in our serviced apartment and we had to eat all three meals outside. Initially it was difficult. But after some time, I started to enjoy it. When I went to a food court and other places, I had the opportunity to interact with different people. I tried different foods. It created such an interest in me and made me curious about the varieties of ingredients you could put into your food. I tasted different foods from different parts of the world, from Chinese food to European food. Oh, it was not bad after all." But eventually, they found their own place and resumed cooking their own meals at home.

She immediately felt at home, "What I felt is that people are more welcoming here. They are very comfortable with the English language. With the local Chinese community and the Malays, English is very well spoken. Language is never a barrier. Even the Indian community here—there are so many Indians that you don't feel you are away from home."

Her warmth and openness to her new home allows her to instantly make friends with Indians, Chinese, Malay, and other expats from the UK and the US. She tells me, "I feel at home with everyone. It doesn't feel different when I'm with a Chinese or with a Malay." She credits it to an openness of the society as well. She continues: "It's not only an effort on my part. I feel they are really open to be friends with me. I feel good about it." And she would have it no other way, "Today, we are really settled. I am very happy here and it's a nice place for my children to grow up. Even for us, it is safe and secure. We are very happy."

The ease and efficiency is agreeable to this pleasant Indian lady. "One thing very good about Singapore is that the directions are quite clear. Whether you are driving on the roads or taking the MRT, all the signs and directions are in English, so getting around is not a problem. Also, I find people very helpful. When you lose your way, you can always find someone to ask for directions or help. People are very kind."

Kiran had taught different grades of students in international schools in India and Hong Kong. Here in Singapore, she has chosen to be a relief teacher, taking over classes when teachers are sick or need to be replaced for one reason or another. Working for the Canadian International School for many years now, she enjoys the arrangement, giving her time for her family and her passion for The Art of Living.

The Art of Living (AOL) is a six-day workshop, totaling 20 hours, with the Sudharshan Kriya as the heart of the practice. This powerful breathing is a tool that helps clear the mind. And repeatedly Kiran insists that words cannot capture this experiential change in her life. She describes it as a beautiful experience that has taught her so much to be calm and relaxed. So sold on the experience, it almost feels like a testimonial on TV, but the sincerity in Kiran's voice is genuine.

She tells me that prior to the course, her mind was cluttered. Then her daughter Simran smiles. I probe, "Is it true? Did your mom really change?" She confirms it, "Yes, she has changed a lot. A LOT! Before, because my mother does everything 100 percent, so if anything is left undone, she worries about it 100 percent. After AOL, there are no more worries, she just does things 100 percent."

From being a perfectionist who worried about 101 details, she has let go of worrying. Instead, Kiran only gives her best. This describes her outlook to life, "When your heart is 100 percent in love and your mind is empty and your hand is 100 percent busy or occupied, you have no regrets. You will have no complaints. You will not feel sorry for what happens. You will not be anxious."

She then uses the example of a child being fully present when eating an ice cream cone. "We can learn easily from a little child eating an ice cream who is 100 percent present in the activity, with it melting on his clothes. This is what Sudahrino Krisha teaches."

She then explains, "The Art of Living is about the breath. It is all we have. But how many of us are consciously aware of that? We have to be consciously aware of our breath, to be able to work on our breath. It's in the mind, we are able to control our mind."

Kiran took the class five years ago, and started teaching the class a year and a half ago.

The guy I was dating was one of her students. She tells me how she remains connected to her students even after the class is over. One of her joys is seeing her students' faces shift from worry on the first day of class to peaceful, relaxed big smiles on the last day.

Her entire family has taken the Art of Living. They continue to practice the meditation daily and are reaping the benefits of it. Her son, studying for his international baccalaureate exam, is unusually calm and relaxed. And her daughter is an extremely mature 23-year-old, who is focused on more important things in life. She blew me away with her wisdom on living abundantly. While many people her age are busy acquiring the latest fashion or material things, she believes otherwise, "If you already feel you have a lot, then a lot will come to you. And if you feel you don't have enough, then you will never have enough. The contentment, self-love, gratefulness, satisfaction, it makes you happy wherever you are."

She admits that she still likes fashion and the latest accessories, but she does not cling to it. "I will be the first to admit I like the latest fashion. I like the latest accessories. When you see a beautiful dress in the shop, you want to possess it. Your mind clings to the thought of acquiring that dress. But you are limiting your own experience. How many dresses can your mind remember? You cannot cling to possessing all the beautiful dresses you see."

Her wise words are true. The wisdom of abundance and not clinging are definitely characteristics of a deeply mindful person. Often people her age have not reached such profound enlightenment. Beaming, Simran's proud mother states, "I can say with confidence that anywhere we go, we are confident we will not be shaken by the events around us."

I point out that I find it interesting how she has found clarity and peace in a place where there is much stress and a strong drive to acquire more money and material things. Kiran explains her mindset: "The thing is how rich is rich? It is entirely up to you. At what point will you be satisfied? You may have a car, but someone may have a more exclusive car than you. Where do you draw the line?" Her mindfulness has made her richer, "I have always been content. I feel blessed. Like today we have a car, but before this we didn't have one. We were happy then, and we are happy now."

Her contentment allows her to enjoy what Singapore has to offer, even happily sharing it with Indian friends and family when they come to visit. She takes them to the Bird Park, to Sentosa, Orchard Road, Clarke Quay, Boat Quay and what the Indian community calls "the Temple". She explains, "Many people call Mustafa a temple because it is so big. When I came in 1984, it was a tiny shop. Now you can get everything under one roof. It is very easy to shop there."

Her family members all have Permanent Resident status in Singapore. When I ask Kiran if this is now her home, she replies, "We bought our own place a year age. We also have a place in Bombay. At this point we're still not sure. We are here because my husband's job brought us here. Right now, we are happy. We don't know how long we will live here, but we are open to anything."

All of a sudden, all the other questions I want to ask about Singapore don't really matter. For this woman is fully present and content with the reality she has. As I listen to her, a clarity comes upon me. Consistent with all the wisdom I have learned from books by Eckhart Toelle, Wayne Dyer, Byron Kathie, and numerous Oprah soul series episodes, plus my zen guru Sr. Sonia, the Buddhist nun, it becomes crystal clear.

The past and future do not matter and all that matters is the present. This pilgrim on a journey is very grateful for the revelation. I thank them profusely for sharing their time with me. The wise mother and daughter leave the café and I am abundantly filled with an openness of the joy and beauty of what my life now offered. And right now, my reality is to joyfully be in Singapore.

Part

III

EPILOGUE

One year, seven months, and seven days from my big move to Singapore, I found myself on an airplane to Denver, Colorado, via Tokyo and Los Angeles. Being up in the sky and on a journey always makes for the perfect setting for gaining some perspective in my life, giving me time and space to process my current reality, as well as an opportunity to prepare for the next adventure I will embark on.

I was going to the US for 46 days to attend a conference of international culinary professionals in Denver, to secure more food and travel writing opportunities, and to attend my eldest sister's wedding. Lost in my thoughts, I was interrupted by the graceful sashay of the tall and lean flight attendant wearing the flattering blue *kebaya* visually associated with the airline. I fixed my gaze on their hairdos, realizing they all had the same side-swept bangs and the same bun holding up their locks with a noticeable amount of hairspray. I thought about how laborious it would be, while also acknowledging that it came with the package and many men around the world find these flight attendants beautiful and elegant. I have yet have to see a chubby Singapore Airline flight attendant. Surely, the airline has managed to market the image of the lovely Asian woman, providing the best service on the world's best airline.

The flight to Tokyo was not fully booked. Except for a child who appeared autistic, occasionally shrieking with a shrill voice, the airplane was otherwise silent. I looked out of the window and sighed with relief. The past few days leading up to my trip had been hectic. This would be the longest time I will be away from Singapore since I had moved here.

To be away for 46 days was a long time. I aptly bid my friends goodbye, sending messages to them. But to mark my going away, my dearest friend Emmanuel planned a relaxing Sunday with me before I left. We agreed to meet at Wheelock Place along Orchard Road at 12 noon. I usually stay away from Orchard on Sundays as it is packed to the brim, but we would make an exception this time for the Thai bazaar held in the Thai Embassy right smack in the center of town. I breezed out of the Orchard MRT station. As I stood waiting for the traffic light to change so I could cross the street to reach Wheelock Place, the guy on my left looked at me. To my surprise it was Emmanuel. We burst into laughter at how we had mastered orchestrating our rendezvous in the city. On several occasions, we had managed to meet up on specific trains or buses as everything runs like clockwork here.

It was a hot Sunday. I was clad in a white airy sundress and my comfy flip flops, while Emmanuel was dressed in a coordinated beige top, beige plaid shorts, and a chocolate brown leather thong. We headed to the Thai bazaar, going straight to the food section. Booths serving *phad thai,* green mango salad, papaya salad, *tom yum goong,* olive rice, pineapple fried rice, chicken wings, tako, and other native desserts all appeared appetizing. In true Singaporean style,

Emmanuel quickly got us a table by using one of the Thai Embassy brochures to reserve a seat. I bought us each a plateful of *phad thai*, while he bought chicken wings. With the freshly cooked, sweetish spicy flavour of the rice noodles, shrimps, bean sprouts, and egg all joyfully blended in my mouth, we relaxed and enjoyed our lunch. A Filipino man joined us at our round table for four. An engineer who recently moved to work in Singapore, he told us about his daughters back home. Like many, he thought Emmanuel and I were husband and wife. But he initially hesitated to converse with me, thinking I was Singaporean. After our meal, a Bangladeshi man quickly cleared our table and we stayed on to catch up on more stories, as another Filipino couple joined us at the table. For dessert, we shared sticky rice with mangoes. Every bite of the chewy rice drizzled with coconut cream, and the natural sweetness of the mango made us even more content than we already were.

Then in our blissful state, we surveyed every single booth selling jewelry, clothes, and accessories from Thailand. I purchased a lovely pair of sterling silver dangling earrings, a sparkling floral brooch, and a black silk shawl hand painted with strokes of silver and gold. And for a change, this Sunday I was not weighed down with my signature heavy bag and laptop. My back appreciated the respite and was desperate for a massage. Prior to meeting Emmanuel, I asked if we could go to Little India to try the cheap massage his friend recommended, or any other affordable yet decent massage place we could find. Little did I know that my dear friend had planned a surprise for me. He made reservations with a Chinese massage specialist for a choice of a foot or back massage in a shop in Shaw Tower. We hopped on the bus from Orchard, getting off at Raffles Hotel, then walked a few blocks to Shaw Tower. I loved this part of town for it reverberated with fond memories—First Thai, a small hole in the wall Thai restaurant I loved along Purvis Street, and the decadent experience of sitting by the sunbed at Naumi Hotel's rooftop infinity pool.

I made a quick stop to the Ladies' Room before getting a massage. When I returned, my friend was seated on the back massage chair, grunting in relief from the intense rubbing. With all three men at work, I waited for my turn. The most cheerful of the three masseuse greeted me "*Ni Hao?*" I then politely told them I don't speak Chinese. He smiled and continued rubbing his customer's feet. When it was my turn, my very tight back and shoulders got the attention they needed. A Chinese doctor, who only spoke a few words in English, repeatedly told me "Relax", while working his magic on my tense body.

Continuing our adventure, Emmanuel and I then hopped on the MRT to Raffles Place to take advantage of the free entrance to an ongoing exhibit of The Kangxi Emperor: Treasures from the Forbidden City at the Asian Civilisations Museum. There was an unbelievable queue of people, with frail grandparents patiently waiting in line, young toddlers in prams, and every one else in between. The line snacked between three galleries, moving inch by inch. My stay in Singapore had taught me patience in following queues and this was perhaps the biggest test of it. After some thirty minutes or so, we breezed through the showcase of relics from one of China's greatest emperors. By the time we were ready to leave, it was no longer hot outside. The rain was now pouring. Hungry from our adventure, we deemed it apt to head back to the Thai embassy for beef ball soup and *tom yum goong*.

After more than a year and a half in this island, there are still opportunities for new experiences in Singapore, from a traditional

Chinese massage to a lesson in the culture of the Chinese, to authentic cuisine from neighboring Thailand.

When the airplane reached Tokyo, all passengers had to disembark, with the passengers continuing to Los Angeles to return to the plane an hour later. To my delight, the seat next to me remained empty, and it was still the same guy sitting one seat away. He was already sitting down when I arrived with my camera bag, carry-on bag, handbag, and laptop. My pleasantries soon turned into a long conversation. He turned out to be a Singaporean en route to Las Vegas for a conference. In his late thirties, he was working in sales, a job he did not enjoy. He was a third generation Filipino residing in Singapore, with his grandfather working as a musician in Singapore many decades ago when all the Filipinos in this island knew each other. Educated in the US and with a love for travel, plus his laid-back personality and English sans the Singlish accent, I wouldn't have picked him out as a Singaporean. I divulged more about myself and my life than I probably should have, including details of my last semblance of romance. He openly shared his aborted love story too. While we did not know anyone in common, he was thrilled to learn that I sing in the church he was baptized in and where his parents still attend mass religiously every Sunday. He lived in a colonial-style black and white house in Portsdown Road, a suburb quickly becoming hip and popular among expats with cars. He openly shared how cheap his rent was. Learning I am a writer and an artist, he repeated over and over that I should move to Bali, Indonesia. He was not the first to make this suggestion to me. The island after all has a large community of artists, painters, writers, and a very strong bohemian vibe. Add to that the setting is lovely, and the cost of living is much cheaper than Singapore. This airplane seatmate of mine boldly made the forecast that he did not see me living in Singapore for a long time. In one or two years, he wanted to join his French buddy from university and move to Bali. But right now, he was stuck in a job in sales, which he had to do to earn his living. As a compromise, he would frequently travel around Asia, often to Indonesia, where he had a long love affair with a Muslim woman. The woman had gotten married. He is now dating another Muslim woman. But being a Catholic and a pork eater, he is not sure if their relationship will go anywhere. In the meantime, he is never in Singapore for longer than two months without a quick getaway to nearby Southeast Asian destinations.

As the lights in the plane were dimmed and many passengers began amusing themselves with over a hundred entertainment options available on the mini TV screens in front of them, I briefly pondered my seatmate's suggestion of moving to another place. But in my heart, I knew I was not ready to leave Singapore yet.

Arriving in LAX, I walked from the gate to a construction maze leading us to the immigration officers. Compared to Changi Airport's gloriously tidy and organized layout, this was a nightmare. The vents and the electrical wires dangled from the ceiling. There was a formal immigration procedure where you had to scan your fingers and thumbs, and also capture an image of your eye. A Labrador and a Belgian Mallinoise surveyed passengers' bags as we waited for the checked in suitcases to make their way out of the plane onto the revolving carousel. I had forgotten how much small talk played a role in everyday interactions in America. Pushing my trolley of suitcases through customs, the officer asked why I wasn't stopping at Los Angeles. I candidly answered that I had no friends in LA. "I can be your friend," he flirtingly replied. Never would I get that from anyone working in Singapore's airport, or perhaps in any Singapore government agencies.

Moving to the domestic terminal required a long walk outside the airport, passing several cab drivers, and frightening characters standing around the terminal. I was then appalled to see a long queue at the check in area. With only a handful of personnel, it was all computerized check in. But there was a glitch with my ticket, caused by using a different credit card, and I had to join the long queue waiting for the assistance from the handful of United Airlines personnel present. More than twenty minutes later, I had to endure another long queue to get through the x-ray screening of my carry-on bags. I was wiped out, hungry, and sweaty by the time I reached the gate for my flight.

Culture Shock

Twenty-five hours after I had left the comforts of my lovely condominium in Far Horizon Gardens, I finally arrived in Denver. With temperatures averaging 40°F when I arrived, the black bulky coat my dear German friend Alex lent me came in handy. Not wanting to spend a fortune on a cab ride from the airport, and fearful that the cab driver would take me for a ride, I settled on an airport van shuttle. Along with six other conference participants consisting of food professionals and psychologists, we drove to downtown Denver in animated conversation. Strangers quickly became comfortable acquaintances. But as we neared the city, a silence fell upon us as we saw a long line of homeless extending over a block long. Thirty or so people were queuing up to get a bed and some warmth in this shelter on this especially cold night in April.

I was shocked for during my whole time in Singapore, I had only encountered a homeless person once. I was on my way to a lunch meeting with my Canadian editor at Amoy Street in Chinatown. Walking by the URA building, I saw a man sitting on the floor looking scruffy and dirty. "I saw a bum," were the first words I told my editor in disbelief, as I had been in Singapore for a year before this happened. Perhaps the excitement was not appropriate, but it was more a reflection of how poverty was something I did not have to see head on in Singapore. The sight of the homeless shelter in Denver brought me back to the reality of poverty in the world.

In the five nights I spent in Denver, I began to deeply appreciate the comfortable and warm living conditions Singapore afforded me. The Mile High city had a free mall shuttle that plied through 16th Street. The conference was held in the Sheraton, some four blocks away from my cozy boutique hotel, but it required passing though the Walgreens in the corner of my street, where there were always shady male characters congregating. Making eye contact easily resulted in awkward conversations. Even inside the shuttle bus, some odd characters did not hesitate to strike up a conversation whether you liked it or not. The funny thing is that I often faulted Singaporeans for not smiling or making small talk. Yet as I gingerly negotiated this foreign American city, how I wished I were in Singapore in my little bubble, not needing to deal with strange characters. Walking from the Sheraton Hotel to the Convention one afternoon along with Alona, a Venezuelan-American lady from Florida, we reached the traffic intersection. The stoplight clearly indicated the red man, which meant that pedestrians had to stop. She was puzzled why I stopped when it was obvious there were no cars. I explained, "In Singapore, you can get caught for jaywalking." At that moment, I realized I had become a stickler for rules. I went on telling her, "In fact in Singapore, there are people who can stop smokers and check the cigarette to see if it had the tax stamp to confirm if they had paid duty for it, or illegally smuggled it in." She appeared slightly shocked.

Later in my stay in Denver, I saw a man throw a cigarette butt on the street, quickly extinguishing the light with a quick movement of his shoe. I was appalled, for it had been a long time since I had last seen someone litter.

After five nights, on my last day in Denver, I struggled with 20°Farenheit temperatures. I innately had an adventurous spirit and an intense hunger to savor what the new place had to offer. But in this case, battling the freezing cold and mingling with strange bystanders on the street was too much for a single Asian woman to deal with. I resorted instead to quickly grabbing a bite in a nearby Mexican grill, then curling up in a cozy chair in my hotel to wait for the airport shuttle to pick me up.

At the airport, as I patiently stood in line waiting for my turn to get a boarding pass to Philadelphia, I noticed a man chewing gum. Prior to my move to Singapore, there was always a pack of gum in my bag. I thoroughly enjoyed relieving the tension in my jaws as I chewed away. But as I gazed at the man happily chewing his gum, I realized I could buy gum in this country, but did not feel the compulsion to do so. My attention now shifted to the cute men in the queue. Thinking to myself, "Wow, who would have thought there would be so many good-looking men in Denver." I then remembered what many of my female friends in Singapore had warned me about. They noticed that when you arrive in Singapore, you will see only a few cute guys. Many call it a drought. But the longer you stay, your standards decline and you will start finding mediocre-looking guys to suffice. I wondered if this was what happening to me in the Denver Airport. Had I been in Singapore for too long?

One thing became clear—Singapore has made a dent on me. The land without chewing gum has become my home. Surely it has its quirks: the reserving of tables with tissue packs and oft-incomprehensible Singlish, chatty "uncles" driving cabs, a society so engrossed with shopping, portable video games, iPods, and tinkering with their mobiles and blackberries. I no longer smile or say good morning to every person I see when I go on my morning walk. I also don't expect strangers to be warm or engage in small talk with me in the MRT or cafes.

But what it has given me is a safe and comfortable setting to explore varied cultures and cuisines. The Chinese, Malay, and Indian cultures are just a few of Singapore's many offerings. More importantly, it allows me to joyfully celebrate the global citizen I am. I will always be a Filipino at heart. But I have embraced belonging to a bigger community of people. In the company of many expats in Singapore, I have found myself. Many wonderful people have opened their souls to me, allowing a deep connection and friendship to blossom. Many of them have journeyed with me, and generously trusted me with their stories.

As you may now know, there is no typical expatriate in Singapore. Each one has a unique story to tell. And as many of my friends have learned and echoed over and over in these pages, it is in leaving and taking frequent trips overseas that one appreciates Singapore more. I have only been away for a week, but I have already scribbled in my journal many things I want to do when I get back. Right now, I am craving for a big bowl of spicy Katong *laksa* with cockles. I would happily trade this cold weather for the constancy of hot and humid days. I look forward to sighing, "I'm home," when my plane touches down in Changi Airport. And I delight in more adventures and more relationships waiting to unfold in Singapore.

When I had last seen Sr. Bubbles in Manila, I shared all the stories of my stint in Singapore. As a friend and a wise spiritual director, she listened intently to the details of my life. This spunky nun and accomplice to the food trip two years ago that started it all then look at me knowingly, and she said, "You know, all these years I had known you were meant for Singapore."

About the Author

Maida Pineda is creatively committed to savor the golden delicious moments of life. For the past eleven years, she has poured her energy into her passions: food, travel, writing, and food styling. No two days are alike for Maida, as she may be on a mission to discover a new island getaway in the Philippines, bonding with fishermen or farmers, capturing how traditional dishes are made, stalking a *balut* vendor, getting a decadent massage in Thailand, eating her way on the Orient Express from Thailand to Singapore, delighting in hawker food, or whipping a culinary creation in her kitchen. She has written hundreds of magazine articles for fine publications like Singapore Airlines' *Silver Kris*, *Business Traveller*, *Destinasian*, *Timeout Singapore*, Tiger Airways' *Tiger Tales*, Cebu Pacific's *Smile Magazine*, *The Philippine Daily Inquirer*, and *The Philippine Star*. She has also written scripts for television in the early days of Lakbay TV, a travel cable channel devoted to the Philippines' 7,100 islands. Maida is the author of the book *Do's and Don'ts in the Philippines*, a cultural etiquette guide.

Maida has a Master of Arts Degree in Gastronomy from Le Cordon Bleu and the University of Adelaide, and a liberal arts degree from the prestigious Smith College in Massachusetts, USA. Born in Philippines, she has traveled all around the archipelago. She has lived in the US and Australia, and is now based in Singapore. Her big dream is to eat her way around the world.

You may see more of her work at www.maidastouch.com, and follow her decadent adventures at www.themaidastouch.blogspot.com.